ERIC SYKES

OF SEBASTOPOL TERRACE

This book is dedicated to the late
Hattie Jacques and Richard Wattis.
It would be hard to fail with
such brilliant, understanding and
caring people.

ERIC SYKES
OF SEBASTOPOL TERRACE

ERIC SYKES

M & J Hobbs/Michael Joseph
LONDON

ACKNOWLEDGEMENTS

In acknowledgement and grateful thanks to Johnnie Speight, Frank Muir and Dennis Norden, without whose help there would not be such a place as Sebastopol Terrace, nor the characters who made the place live.

Also to my friends at the BBC – Denis Main Wilson, Sidney Lotterby, Philip Barker and especially Roger Race, the Producers and their staffs who helped to make the television series a most enjoyable and successful venture.

To Bill Cotton and Duncan Wood, who brought back the series after a short absence, enabling us to complete twenty years, which I believe is a record. Unfortunately, the record is not on sale, as nobody asked us to make one.

To all the actors and actresses who worked on the show.

First published in Great Britain by M & J Hobbs,
55 Wellington Close, Hepworth Way,
Walton-on-Thames, Surrey and Michael Joseph Ltd,
44 Bedford Square, London WC1B 3EF
1981

ISBN 0 7181 2081 7

Typeset by Cambrian Typesetters, Farnborough
printed by Hollen Street Press, Slough and
bound by Hunter & Foulis, Edinburgh

CONTENTS

Hat on the horns of a dilemma: 'Is your brother an idiot or isn't he?'

POSTMEN

Millions of people post letters every day without incident, and I suppose most postmen are reasonable, ordinary, every-day people, but there's always the awkward one, and when I set out to post a letter you can bet your sweet life that it's the awkward one who is emptying the box at that moment . . . It was. As I dashed up the street, he was just locking the box with an enormous bunch of keys that would have given a normal man a hernia. He turned to face me and I held out my letter.

'What's that for?' he said, slinging the bag over his shoulder.

'It's a letter.'

He paused to light the remains of a fag; then he said: 'I can see it's a letter. I've been on this job for nearly two years now and I can spot a letter immediately. What are you giving it to me for?'

'Well, you're a postman.'

'What's that got to do with it?' he said.

I didn't really know how to answer that – after all, it wasn't as if I'd asked him for half a dozen lamb chops – so I just stood there looking at him.

'All you have to do,' he said, as if he was talking to an idiot child, 'you put your letter in that little slot . . .', he paused to let this sink in, '. . . in the side of the box. OK?'

Now inevitably, when I find myself in a spot like this, a

crowd always seems to gather, and there they were – two scruffy little urchins who'd obviously heard the postman's last remark because one of them pointed helpfully to the slot. I could feel myself going red, especially as the other little ratbag tried to take the letter from me in order to post it. I pulled away from him.

'I know how to post a letter,' I said. The two lads looked at each other and giggled. The postman waited patiently. He said, 'It won't bite you.'

'Yes,' I said, 'but you've just emptied it.'

'Well then,' he replied, 'there'll be plenty of room for yours, won't there,' and with that he started to stuff the bag into his van.

At this point I should have tossed the letter into the box, winked at the lads and made some kind of sarcastic remark about the Post Office, but I never seem to think of the obvious. I certainly wasn't going to be humiliated by this spotty herbert in a postman's uniform – a typical youth of today with a few sparse hairs on his top lip which I suppose he thought made him look macho; it was pathetic – I've had girlfriends with a better growth than that. Anyway the thing had gone too far for me to back down in front of these two kids, but what was I to do? Perhaps if I handed him the letter with a pound note, in such a way that they couldn't see it . . . but I rejected that idea straight away, I didn't have a pound on me, and even if I had he'd probably hold it up for all the world to see, and say 'What's this, then' . . . He was still sorting stuff out in the back of his van, and I thought of leaning in to tell him confidentially that it was an urgent letter to my mother in hospital who had only a few days to live. No, I wasn't going to grovel, also the two kids had moved forward with their ears hanging out and I didn't want them to know about my mother. In any case she'd been dead for twenty years. I looked at the postman. What I should do was shove him up against his van, and say 'Now listen Buster', but he wasn't all that small, and with my luck he'd turn out to be a judo black belt. So I appealed to his better nature . . . .

I smiled, 'Come on lad, you could just slip it into your bag.'

He slammed the door, and locked it. 'Yes, I suppose I could, and supposing everybody started giving me letters, what would happen to these pillar boxes, they'd be useless, no good to anybody apart from the odd dog.' Then he got in his van and started the engine.

I bent down to the window. 'Where's the next box?' I shouted.

He leaned across. 'The next one's in Balaclava Road.'

'Balaclava Road,' I said, 'that's just around the corner. Give me five minutes' start.'

'Hop in,' he said. 'I'll give you a lift', and he opened the door.

'Thanks,' I said, and looked triumphantly to the lads, but they were already racing down the street.

'We have regulations, you know,' shouted the postman over the noise of the engine, 'and we have to abide by them.' He didn't seem to be a bad fellow after all.

'I appreciate that,' I shouted back. 'If we didn't have rules we'd be all over the place, so I can see your point of view, and I wouldn't have bothered you like this, only this letter is rather important . . . . It's to my mother in hospital, and I only hope it reaches her in time . . . .'

'What you on about?' he said, and I realized he hadn't heard a word . . . .

It's a sad world, it really is. Here's this young fellow: he's got his health, a good job in the Post Office, and a nice little van to run around in, so he couldn't care less about the elderly. But I cared. I could see them dashing to the bedside . . . a letter from your son . . . I knew he would not let me down, and a tear would trickle down the wrinkled old cheek . . . I blew my nose, looked down at the envelope in my hand, and came back to earth with a bump

– 'Goal of the Month, c/o *Grandstand,* BBC' . . . . I shoved it in my pocket in case he saw it.

We pulled up at the pillar box just as the two kids arrived, red and breathless but eager to watch developments. I nipped out and pushed the letter into the box. He was still in the van, leaning across to watch me.

'There you are,' he said. 'It's easy, isn't it?'

I waited by the box, and he went to wind up the window.

'Hang on,' I said, 'aren't you going to empty it?'

'No,' he said, 'I did that one first.' And with that he drove off.

For a moment there was stunned silence, then the kids turned and dashed off in high glee to spread the news round the neighbourhood.

CIRCUMSTANTIAL EVIDENCE

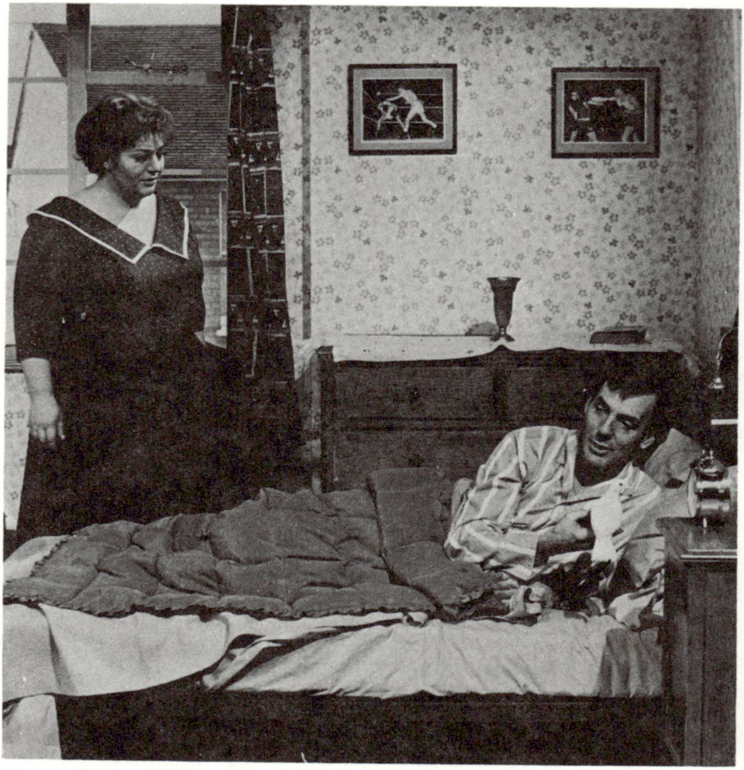

Hat and me with Muriel and Norman. Norman is the bed.

I was once held by the police on suspicion of murder. Never again. Take my advice and stick to having no dog licence or road fund tax disc, but don't get arrested on suspicion of murder because it's too much of a hassle. However, if you should be unfortunate enough to have your collar felt, make sure they don't find the body, because without it they're stymied. There must be Habeas Corpus. So it was with me – they couldn't find the body. But in my case it was because the body was still living, and it's no good the police digging up gardens, testing the ash in the boiler, and taking samples from the bath if the body is alive and well with a large gin and tonic in its hand, all unaware that it's supposed to be the body. However we'll come to that later; let me tell you how it all began . . . .

I woke up one morning with the feeling that all was not as it should be. I turned my head towards the alarm clock – it hadn't gone off, but then it was a very indifferent alarm; many's the time I've had to wake up and bang it before it would ring. Why I bothered to wind it up every night I don't know – it only had one hand – but it wasn't that. A movement caught my eye. I looked up suddenly and there, perched on the bed rail, was a dove. It was looking at me with its head on one side and doing a little side shuffle along the rail. A dove. Yes, a real live dove, pure white, and there it was on my bed rail; but why had it come to me? Noah had a dove land on his boat but as far as I can recollect there wasn't much else in the world it could have landed on. I believe in the mysterious ways of the universe and some force greater than us must have sent that dove, but again – why me? Mind you, if I'd known the trouble that bird was to cause me I'd have flattened it with a cricket bat there and then.

I slid out of bed so I wouldn't frighten it, and gently started to take off my pyjamas. Not only was the bird unafraid, but it fluttered on to the bedside table to get a better look. Well, I suppose there are lots of people who don't mind being watched by a bird when they get dressed, but I'm not one of them. In any event I went behind the wardrobe door to put my underpants on – silly, I suppose, but it's the way I've been brought up.

Now for those of you who don't know, I live with my sister Hattie. Well we're twins actually, although we've grown into very different-shaped people, but as I'm slim I make it a rule never to talk about her size – so I won't mention it. Anyhow, I couldn't wait to see the look on her face when I walked downstairs with a real live dove perched on my finger, and I wasn't disappointed.

She came out of the kitchen with a teapot in her hand, and stopped dead in her tracks as if she'd hit a brick wall. 'What are you doing up so early? It's not ten o'clock yet.' As she spoke tea was pouring out of the spout on to the floor. 'Oh, now look what you've made me do,' she said. 'Go and get a cloth.'

'It's a dove, Hat. Look', I said.

'I can see it's a dove. I'm not blind. What are you doing with it?'

'It was on my bed rail when I woke up.'

'On your bed rail?'

'Yes, just above my head.'

'It must have come through the window.'

'Yes.'

'It's funny, that.'

'It is really, when you come to think of it.'

'Was it raining last night?'

'The weathermen said there was a low coming in from the Azores.'

'I'll put the kettle on.' And with this she swept into the kitchen . . . .

It's surprising really, the amout of time and energy Hat and I spend on useless dialogue, but that's life. If people didn't make stupid remarks all the time there wouldn't be much conversation at all, so I suppose one mustn't grumble – which is precisely the kind of remark I'm talking about. As we ate breakfast the bird perched on the toast rack, having a go at the toast when it thought we weren't looking, and I started to tell Hat in detail how I'd woken up to find the bird on the bed rail. It was four o'clock in the afternoon before Hat finally grasped the events of the morning, which means either that my explanations are getting more lucid or that Hat is becoming more perceptive.

During the next couple of days Hat became reconciled to the fact that the bird was no casual visitor but a regular boarder; indeed she was the one who christened it Muriel, because she's always been good with names – for instance Peter for the cuckoo clock, Jaws for the goldfish. There was a time when she wanted to call the settee Ernest, but I soon quashed that. I mean, there's no end to it once you start that lark – everything has to have a name.

'Where's my socks?'

'I've put 'em in Wilfred and you look in the drawer.'

'Not Nellie, Wilfred's upstairs next to Albert.'

That's the straight road to madness.

However, getting back to Muriel, the dove, she couldn't just do as she pleased if she was determined to stay; she had to be trained, and I haven't watched the Barbara Woodhouse programmes for nothing. I know she's dogs, but it's basically the same. However, I felt there was a rapport between Muriel and me; after all she had perched on my bed. I know whose bed I'd perch on if I had half a chance, but then that's another story. Anyway, I felt she shouldn't be too difficult to train. I tied a little bell on the bed rail, and she watched me, head cocking from side to side, and she cooed, which I wrote down, because it obviously meant 'What's that?' I pointed to it and said 'Bell', and she cooed again, but it sounded exactly like the coo she did for what's that, so I decided to leave verbal communications for later.

Lesson One: first of all I hit the bell with my head, then ate a piece of corn, and then I hit the bell with my head again, and ate another piece of corn, and all the time the bird watched me quizzically. The message was simple – hit the bell and you get some corn . . . even a stupid bird should be able to understand that. With infinite patience I demonstrated again and again, but it was useless. I can now only surmise that the bird hated corn or else it had a secret stock of food on the side, but either way it refused to ding the bell. After a week of this I gave up; I not only had a lump the size of an egg over one eye, I was constipated as well.

I only wish the same could be said for Muriel, because this was the start of the trouble – for a little dove she made a terrible mess all over everything. She not only had bowels, but her feathers wouldn't stay in. Hat of course spent hours scrubbing and polishing and chipping, but no sooner had she got the house reasonably clean than whoosh . . . Muriel was flying about dropping stuff all over again. But you can't put a bird out every night like a cat, or take it for a walk round the block like a dog. Muriel wasn't dim, though – in fact she was very good at one trick. I had her on my finger, then with a hup I flipped her in the air, and she'd stand on my head. This was dangerous for obvious reasons, but the crunch came when she got her feet entangled in my hair, panicked and nearly lifted me upstairs, so I never did that again.

By now you are wondering what this dove has to do with me being on a suspected murder charge. Well, I'm coming to that.

By this time Hat's patience was running out; she was barely civil to the bird, and one day it happened – one of those tiny links in the chain of inevitable disaster. It was twenty past three in the afternoon when Peter the cuckoo clock decided to cuckoo. I was just checking my watch, and as Peter came out for the fifth time the dove, supposed to be a symbol of peace mind you, attacked it. Well Hat went mad, and as she lunged at the dove with a rolled-up newspaper Muriel did what one might expect her to do when afraid, and Hat, having just spent three hours at the hairdresser's, was underneath. That was the straw that broke the camel's back, and in tears she delivered her ultimatum.

'Either that bird goes or I do.' Then she stormed upstairs to wash her hair. At least that's what I thought, but when she came down again she had her overcoat on and a suitcase in her hand.

'Where are you going?' I said.

'Never you mind, and don't come crawling to me when this house is filthy.'

'Suppose you get a letter, where will I send it?'

'I don't get letters,' she said, full of self-pity.

'Ah yes, but when people know you've gone they'll write to you to find out why.'

'In that case get that filthy bird to deliver it.' With that she bundled out of the door.

I wasn't unduly worried. I knew Hat better than she knew herself – she'd be back in a couple of hours saying she'd forgotten her nightie, or don't forget the gasman's coming tomorrow, or some pretext that would have me pleading with her to stay, then she'd gradually weaken and agree, but not before I'd gone and got rid of that bird, given up my club night, seen to the guttering, and she might even have a go at my smoking. No, I knew her only too well . . . so it was a matter of no little surprise to me that she was still absent three days later, and no word from her.

In those three days the house got into a shocking state, but I couldn't bring myself to get rid of the bird – well, not completely. I came to a compromise. I decided to plant a tree in the front garden so that the bird could live out, as it were, but come in for meals etc., and if the tree was high enough I'd be able to lie in bed and keep an eye on her through the bedroom window. Having come to this decision I forged another link in the chain of circumstances. I should have gone out and bought a tree, but no, I had to be clever. I decided to take a tree from Hyde Park – I reasoned that I could select one just about the right height and transplant it in my garden; even if it died it would still have branches, and Muriel wouldn't really mind if it was a dead tree, as long as it had good footholds.

Not many people would think of taking a fairly large tree from Hyde Park and getting away with it, but then you're not me. Oh yes – there's more to me than meets the eye. I often think that, had I been a POW in Colditz during the war, I would have escaped not once but several times. However, that's as may be; the problem now was how to take a tree from Hyde Park, and I must confess that my scheme almost amazed me. It was so simple it took my breath away. First I hired a black jacket, striped trousers and a bowler hat, then with a clipboard under my arm I just strode into the park and started to cut small slivers from trees and make notes. Naturally it wasn't long before this attracted the attention of one of the park keepers. He was an elderly man, and while pretending to pick up litter he followed me at a respectable distance. I had by now found my tree and I walked round it several times with a magnifying glass. Eventually he came up behind me and coughed discreetly. I ignored this approach, pretending to be engrossed in the tree. I even picked up a leaf and put it in an envelope, this turned out to be a master stroke, because he touched his cap, and said:

'Can I be of any assistance Sir?'

I looked him up and down and said: 'In six months' time it could be all over the park.'

He looked around and said, 'Yes Sir, I suppose it could.' He hadn't the foggiest idea what I was on about, but he hadn't long to go before his pension, and he was keeping his nose clean. I beckoned him to me, and looked furtively around to make sure we wouldn't be overheard.

Then I dropped the bombshell: 'Dutch Elm Disease.'

He paled and stepped back in case he should catch some of it, and repeated: 'Dutch Elm Disease.' He obviously wasn't au fait with Dutch or Elm but he understood the word Disease.

Before he could recover I said: 'I want this tree up, roots and all, and placed on one side.'

'Right away,' he said.

I held him back. 'Not now, this must be done after dark – if it gets out we'd have panic. Dutch Elm moves like the clappers – don't even tell your fellow keepers.' He nodded wisely.

'I'll be back tonight,' I said, 'with a ministry hand cart, and with a bit of luck nobody will be any the wiser.'

He looked at the tree, and I could see that the idea of all that digging was beginning to dawn, and his devotion to Hyde Park was wavering. I was in like a shot – I pointed to a giant beech tree and said: 'If that one catches it, you'll have a job – but with this one out of the way we can stop the rot.' He spat on his hands and I knew I had him. Well, that's how I came by the tree, and it was a mistake.

A week went by and still no news from Hat. Where she was I had no idea, unless she had a chap somewhere that I didn't know about, but that was highly unlikely because Hat hasn't had a lot of romance in her life. There was that GI during the war, but he turned out to be a British Army deserter from Bolton. Hat had a bit of money put by for a rainy day, and he turned out to be the rainy day. He pinched her bike as well. So she's always been a little bit wary of men ever since. However, I had other problems to occupy my mind.

The tree was now planted in my front garden, and although it was heavily braced by ropes and stakes it didn't look too bad. The only fly in the ointment was that, after slogging away digging a six-foot hole for it, nearly causing myself permanent internal damage, Muriel had vanished. Can you imagine that – she'd just gone as mysteriously as she had arrived. I couldn't believe it at first. I walked around the house calling her name, whistling, and rattling a biscuit tin, but nothing. Examining some of the white splotches, I realized she hadn't been gone long, but nevertheless she'd gone. So there I was – no Hat, no Muriel, and a very weary-looking tree blocking out the light from the lounge window. To be truthful I wasn't really heartbroken at the loss of Muriel, but I was beginning to miss Hat; I was down to my last two clean plates and the house had a very nasty smell about it. So I was in the middle of writing an advert for a daily woman when the doorbell rang. My first thought was that Muriel was back, which will give you some idea of how besotted I'd become with that bird; but it wasn't Muriel, it was the police. When I say the police I mean Constable Turnbull, and he's about as likely a policeman as me being opening bat for the West Indies. Constable Turnbull was known to all and sundry as Corky, and was well past retiring age, but as he didn't harm anybody and kept his boots shiny it didn't seem christian to discharge him.

'Hello, Corky,' I said.

He didn't reply for a moment, and he didn't take his helmet off, which is always a bad sign. Then he said: 'Constable, if you don't mind.' He teetered to and fro on his heels, and the light flashed on his row of medal ribbons.

He had six of these that looked impressive, but they only meant he'd been at the back in a lot of places. His eyes wandered round the room, but he never turned his back on me. 'The RSPCA wouldn't let you keep a pig in here,' he said, his eyes boring into mine. I edged away. After all, it was no concern of his if I wanted old newspapers all over the place, and empty bean cans, beer bottles and a bucket on the floor. I was entitled to live like this if I so wished and he couldn't touch me for it. I decided to make the point, though, in case a new law had come out that I hadn't noticed.

'This is my home,' I said.

Again he teetered back and forwards. 'Would you say it lacks a woman's touch?' he said.

'Yes, I suppose it does.'

In a flash he thrust his face into mine and said: 'Where's your sister?'

By this time I was getting fed up with people asking after Hat. I mean what about me – I was the one who was the innocent victim. I didn't own a clean shirt and was down to wearing one of Hat's blouses, which made me look like the soloist in St Paul's choir. 'I don't know where she is, she just went, gone, folded her tents and crept off – *arrivederci.* What's it got to do with you anyway?'

He smiled knowingly. 'A minute ago you said it's your home – not our home, why?'

'You don't live here,' I replied. That floored him.

I had it figured out now. All he was interested in was the fact that Hat wasn't here, and when she wasn't here bang went his free breakfasts, his cheese and pickle sandwiches, and pots of tea at all hours of the day and night. Our house was only one of his watering-places, but it was a good one.

Then he really shattered my complacency. Very quietly he spoke, not even looking at me: 'I must tell you that I've applied for a warrant to dig up that tree of yours.' That really shook me – the park keeper must have reported it, or else Corky must have seen me trundling it on the hand cart. Well, it could only be a fine or even seven days, and seven days in the nick would be better than this rat hole; at least I'd get my meals regularly.

'How did you find that out?' I asked.

'Just put two and two together,' he said. He was shaking with excitement as he took out his notebook. 'Oh yes,' he said. 'I'm not just the bumbling bobby that people make out – this could be the climax of a long and distinguished career.' His eyes were gleaming and he was in such ecstasy he could hardly find enough spit to lick his pencil. All because of a measly tree which for all I know *had* Dutch Elm Disease.

'The climax of a long and distinguished career,' I said. 'It's not the great train robbery you know – and I've only done it once.'

He jumped up, shocked 'Gordon Bennett' – he exploded, his glasses beginning to steam over. 'You'll be lucky to get off with twenty years.'

I was staggered . . . everybody knew Corky's views on the leniency of present-day courts. He was all for the return of capital punishment, flogging, and even bringing back the gibbet for football hooligans, but twenty years for stealing a tree . . . . 'Come off it,' I said, 'twenty years . . . it's my first offence.'

He stared at me in amazement: 'Yes,' he said. 'It's your first offence. God knows what you'll do when you get the hang of it. First offence . . . that's typical of you that is. When you go to Blackpool you don't just paddle out to sea, you have to jump off the tower. Well, you've jumped this time my lad.'

I still couldn't take it in.

'Yes, but twenty years, Corky.'

'Yes,' he said, 'and you'll be lucky to get that, and only then if you plead insanity . . . . Incidentally,' he said, and his voice dropped to a conspiratorial whisper, 'that's your best bet. There's a lot of people around here who'll vouch for it . . . . Now come on lad', he said, all brisk again . . . 'chop chop . . . let's get weaving . . . the canteen'll be open in ten minutes.'

I was now more than a little worried. I mean a joke's a joke, but here I was putting a few personal belongings in a bag, closely watched by Police Constable Turnbull. He allowed me to take my shaving gear but refused to let me take a razor, which was stupid – like buying a car with no wheels. I tried to reason with him: 'Listen, Corky,' I said.

He held up his hand and I stopped dead. It was such a definite gesture that I looked round; I thought he was about to wave somebody through. 'I feel it my duty to warn you, sir, that anything you say may be taken down and used in er . . . in er . . . .' he faltered, and moved to the table from which he picked up a pork pie. He sniffed it; 'How long have you had this?' he said.

'I bought it this morning from Madge's bread shop.'

'Oh, yes?' he said. Then he pulled himself together: 'As I was saying, I must warn you that everything you say will be taken down and may be used in evidence against you.' And all the time he was talking, he was munching away at my pork pie. I swear that if he had a choice between promotion and a hot dinner, he'd be hard pushed to make up his mind.

Anyway, that's enough about him. It was me that was in trouble right up to my neck – I only realized *how* deep when I was being questioned at the local police station. They hadn't charged me for anything; I was merely helping with their enquiries. And do you know what those enquiries were? Murder . . . yes, murder. Well that's ridiculous; you can't murder a tree, and in any case, to my knowledge when I left home it was still living. Strangely enough the detective who was asking all the questions never mentioned the tree at all but kept asking about Hat. Was she insured? Was the house in her name? Was I her only relative? I played it cool. Answering only yes and no etc. I'm not a Bogart fan for nothing. All this time Corky stood by the door with his arms folded. Well, he did disappear once, and when he came back there was a bit of egg on his chin. I could see that the detective was uneasy and didn't seem to be getting anywhere; it was Constable Turnbull who had instigated the proceedings, and he had the niggling feeling at the back of his mind that when Constable Turnbull had anything to do with anything the chances of it ending in disaster were infinite.

For my own part I couldn't see where his line of questioning was leading, but on the second day the penny dropped. The detective had obviously been up most of the night, whereas I'd had a fairly good sleep and the best breakfast since Hat had left. Straightaway he started at me.

'Let's stop playing games, shall we?' He put his jacket over the chair back and loosened his tie. He tilted the lamp so that it shone in my face, then he started the questioning. He kept walking round the back of my chair, and to emphasize the point he hit the desk with a heavy ebony ruler. 'So you have no idea at all where she is.' THWACK with the ruler. 'You expect me to believe that?' THWACK. 'I can be a hard man, a very hard man.' THWACK.

I kept my hand off the desk. If that ruler caught me that would be it – I'd never be able to play the violin. I didn't even own a violin and up to now had never had a go on one, but the same night that Hat left home I watched Stephane Grappelli on the television, and to play like that was my next challenge. After all he's seventy years old, and I'm comparatively young. I was just about to walk on stage in a crowded Albert Hall when THWACK – the ruler hit the desk again.

I jerked up: 'Yes father,' I said.

He could see that my thoughts were all over the place, so he took on a softer tone. 'Listen carefully,' he said, 'because I'm going to read to you . . . .' Then he started to read a statement from the milkman.

As I listened the picture fell into place. For two days running the milkman had seen me digging in the garden; I remembered him putting a bottle on the doorstep, then sauntering casually over towards the hole.

'Sister gone away, then?' he said.

'Yes.' He dodged back as I slung a shovelful of earth over his boot.

He edged forward again: 'Funny that, she doesn't usually go away on her own, does she?'

I didn't reply. I was so far down in the hole that I was looking up his trouser leg, and I noticed that, although the weather was quite mild, he still wore long johns.

He jiggled his milk carrier. 'Did you have a row then?' he said.

I leaned on my shovel. I knew he wouldn't go until he had all the facts – he has a big milk round and people rely on him to find out what's going on in the neighbourhood. 'Yes we had a row. Well, a few words,' I said. 'I had this bird, you see.'

'You had a bird living here?' he said.

'She's still here,' I said. 'You see Hat and I . . . .'

But he wasn't listening. He looked round at me: 'That's a big hole you're digging,' he said.

'Yes.'

But before I could finish he had backed away, falling over one of the gnomes in his haste to spread the news. Well, I should have tumbled to what he was thinking, and by the time the story had passed around the variations would be enormous . . . Muriel would be a dolly bird, 38 bust, high heels and a split skirt, and poor old Hat was stuck in the fridge till the hole was ready. I wasn't too wide off the mark . . . the detective then read me a statement from a woman across the street who said she'd heard screams, and two women arguing.

It was ludicrous. 'It couldn't have been two women,' I laughed. 'Muriel was a bird, a dove, a white muck-spreading variety with feathers, and that's why Hat left home. She just left because she couldn't stand cleaning up after it. Unfortunately, the bird's gone too now, so she can't corroborate my statement either.' The detective was unmoved, so I tried again: 'The bird's gone but there's enough evidence spotted around the house to show you where she's been . . . .' I tailed off lamely.

How could I convince him that Hat and me were great pals? As far as I can recollect, we'd only had one serious row in all our lives and that was during the war when they were taking down the railings everywhere in order to make guns and tanks, and Hat sent off my Meccano set. I've often thought that if the rest of the world got on as well as me and Hat, there'd be peace all over . . . no need of passports, and everybody would have a full belly. Me murder her? Kill off the best cook in Sebastopol Terrace? I'm not that thick. Mind you, there's a lot of people I wouldn't mind doing away with, but Hat is the last person in the world . . . with her gone it would be a life of cold beans out of a tin, no buttons on my shirts, holes in my socks. I might even be forced to marry and you can keep that for a lark. Where've you been? Who with? Are you coming to bed? Isn't it time you got up? Yackety yackety yack. Even buttoned up shirts and a good hotpot aren't worth that.

Time went by . . . questions by day and down to my cell for the evenings. It wasn't so bad in there – the food was substantial and there was plenty to read, although some of the stuff on the ceiling was a bit obscure – but the circumstantial evidence was piling up against me. Where was Hat? Scores of detectives were going round interviewing people, showing photos of Hat and asking had they seen her, but nothing turned up. They even showed a picture of her on television, and of course letters came in. She'd been seen on the Holyhead Ferry, in Polperro, in Swansea, all over –

in fact somebody even wrote in to say she was a clippie in Wolverhampton. Hat must have read about it in the newspapers or the telly and she'd be round like a shot to have me out . . . but she didn't come. So where was she? Perhaps she was dead? Suppose she'd fallen off Beachy Head and even now was floating around the Channel, not only unable to help me out of this mess but a danger to shipping as well. It was now eight days since the disappearance and it was beginning to show. Gone was the Bogart image – I was now more like Woody Allen in the middle of a breakdown; my nerves were shot to pieces and I was smoking so much that the Constable would open my cell door in the morning and say 'Are you there?' Strangely enough I wasn't pale due to being under the hard light so long for questioning. Perhaps if I'd had my shirt off during the interrogation you would have thought I was just back from the South of France.

It was on that morning that they decided to take me back to my house to re-enact what had happened on the day Hat left. Well, it made a change, and it would be good to see the outside world again, but I didn't even get that pleasure. They bundled me into a car with a blanket over my head, although it wasn't raining, and I sat like that in the back of the car between two policemen. I suppose they kept the blanket over me so I wouldn't know which police station I'd been at. Anyway the car stopped and I was rushed up the path and into my front door. Then they whipped off the blanket. I couldn't take it in at first – what a shambles, everything had been shifted . . . walls were taken away, and some of the floorboards were gone; there'd been nothing like it since I tried my hand at decorating. Police were all over the place. They were digging out the back and in the front, and I could hear the sound of pickaxes coming from the boiler-room. A big fellow came towards me, then perched on a corner of the table and took out a notebook.

'Right, lad,' he said. 'What were your sister's last words before she . . .' he paused and cleared his throat, '. . . before she went?'

I tried to think – what *did* she say? It's very difficult to remember anything that Hat says since its mostly useless trivia anyway. Then I noticed that the noise of digging had stopped and the pickaxes were silent. The big fellow slowly rose and looked over my shoulder. I turned, and my legs nearly gave way. There was Hat standing in the doorway . . . what a moment. It would have made a marvellous tableau like *When Did You Last See Your Father?* It could only have been a few seconds, but it seemed hours before anybody moved. Then Hat spoke.

'Typical! I turn my back for five minutes and come back to find this.'

I still couldn't believe it. 'It's great seeing you, Hat. We thought you were dead.'

'*Did* you,' she said. 'And the first thing you do is have a party.'

By this time Constable Turnbull, who had been standing in the corner with a beef sandwich, was unobtrusively backing into the kitchen. Some of the diggers were putting their jackets on, and the big fellow looked as if he'd just eaten a 500-year-old oyster. He had a horrific vision of himself directing traffic at Marble Arch. 'Just a moment, madam. I'm Detective-Superintendent Bullshaw.' He wondered fleetingly how much longer he would be able to use that title. 'I take it you are this man's sister?'

'Police,' said Hat. 'What are you doing here? What's happening? I knew I shouldn't have gone away.'

The Superintendent was still trying desperately to salvage something: 'May I ask, madam, why you didn't come forward to our call for information before now?'

'Because,' said Hat, 'the first I knew that anything was wrong was when I turned the corner of the street and saw the crowd.'

I stared at her in amazement. 'You mean you didn't know that the police were looking for you?'

'Looking for me?' said Hat. 'I didn't know they were looking for me. I've done nothing wrong.'

'Yes, but they even showed your picture on television asking for your whereabouts.'

'My picture . . .' Hat's face lit up. 'Where did you get the picture from? I hope it wasn't the one you took of me at Gravesend.'

'Never mind what picture it was.' I was beginning to feel the frustration of the last few days.

Hat was still thinking of that magic moment when the whole nation had been looking at her picture on the television. Then she continued: 'I never saw it because I've been staying with Jessie Crutcher. You know, Eric, Jessie Crutcher she used to sit in front of you at school . . . tall, thin girl with bad eyes, and she had a lot of trouble with boils.'

I still couldn't remember. As a matter of fact I was hard pushed to remember the name of the school.

Hat went on: 'Jessie Crutcher . . . you fancied her at one time.'

Fancied her? It must have been me who had bad eyes. 'OK, OK,' I said. 'What's that got to do with you not coming forward to help the police?'

Hat looked at the policeman as if to say, that's the kind of idiot I have to put up with. 'Because Jessie lives by herself on a farm in Wiltshire and she doesn't have television, nor a radio.'

I couldn't believe it – no television. It's incredible that people in this exciting technological age still prefer to put their head in the sand . . . . How can you live without a television set? How can you join in a conversation if you haven't seen *Coronation Street*, or *Crossroads*? How can one appreciate the history of our island heritage if you haven't watched *Poldark*, not to mention that I now have a smattering of several languages, and possibly if the occasion arose could assist in open heart surgery . . . . And not even a radio for goodness sake – what do they do for the time without the six pips . . . look at the sun?

'And I don't suppose you ever noticed it in the newspapers either,' asked the Superintendent.

'Jessie doesn't get the newspapers.' Hat took her headscarf off and wondered if she put her suitcase down whether it might go through the floor never to be seen again.

I couldn't get over it. Not even newspapers – good grief, what does she light the fire with? And does she know the war's over? Hat said she did but not the last one . . . .

Anyway that was how I beat the rap of suspected murder and it wasn't all black news. We got a tidy sum from the police in compensation, and they even offered to plant a new tree, but I wasn't having that. I've had my fill of country so I told them to put concrete down – it looks just as good painted green and you don't have to mow it. Corky was suspended for a while, but he still walked his beat everyday; now they've let him wear his uniform again and he's being well fed. As far as the Superintendent in charge of the case is concerned he seems to have disappeared off the face of the earth, but my bet is he's odd job man on a lonely farm in Wiltshire.

BURGLARY

It says, 'Be firm, show him who's master.'

We have a fellow living next door to us who's fifty odd years old and a bachelor. Everybody calls him Mr Brown – everybody, that is, unless you happen to be the mayor, or the captain of the golf club, or even if you have a title; then you can call him Charles. We call him Mr Brown. I did suggest to him once that Brown was a common name, but he put up one of his eyebrows, looked at me coldly and said he was one of the Shropshire Browns, so I mentioned casually that I was one of the Lancashire Sykeses, and before he could get back at me Hat was in with a cup of tea, and that quelled another peasant uprising. He's always on about 'us' against 'them'; he's 'us' but Hat and me are definitely third-rate 'thems' so why he's always popping into our house trying to impress us beats me. Hat really thinks he's something special, and if I wasn't there she'd be in his house every morning first thing in a black frock, white apron and a little frilly cap, bobbing and curtseying all over the place . . . .

Anyway another day dawned – well, it had dawned four or five hours ago – and I was sitting up in bed writing to Sophia Loren. I write every week, but she doesn't reply, so a lot of the passion's gone out of it now and it's more or less a duty letter. I was just telling her how my rash had cleared up nicely when Hat burst in.

'Mr Brown's been burgled,' she gasped. 'They did him last night . . . the postman just told me . . . .'

'How much did they get away with?' I asked.

'Well, I dunno,' she said, 'but it must be thousands and thousands.'

I looked at her. She's so impressionable – she reckons Mr Brown's furniture is all Wedgwood and he eats all his meals off genuine Chippendale, but as I keep pointing out to her, if he's landed gentry what's he doing living in Sebastopol Terrace next to a dump like ours? She says there's no disgrace in being impoverished. I'm still trying to figure that one out.

However Hat was upset and all for dashing round to Mr Brown's with a bowl of hot soup; I was worried too – in the past three weeks there had been two other burglaries: next door lower down, and the one next to it. Now, with Mr Brown's, the thought ran through my mind that if they'd really cleaned him out there might have to be a whip round, or worse still Hat might take him in till he got on his feet again. I decided that whatever happened Hat mustn't go and call on him. I know Hat. 'Can we be of any help? And wallop! He'd have his feet under our table so quick she'd still be in his house. He'd get all the treatment. Oh yes. He'd have my bedroom while I would have to make do with the settee, and I'd have to eat with my jacket on. Oh yes, we've had him here before, so I know the score. I dressed in a flash and got downstairs just in time.

Hat was about to slip next door to see if she could do anything – couldn't we take him in till he got sorted out? I soon put a stop to that, and I was in the middle of explaining how they had some very nice institutions for elderly gentlefolk when the doorbell rang. I knew that only Mr Brown could ring our doorbell like that. It didn't make its usual pleasant chime, it was more of a command. In he walked – well he never seems to *walk* in, it's more of an entrance – and I was amazed. I'd expected a broken old man with a blanket round his shoulders, but not a bit of it. He was dressed impeccably as always, handkerchief sticking out of his cuff, and he was beaming all over his face.

'Heard the news, Sykes?' he gushed. 'I've been burgled.'

I was dumbfounded. Here was a man who'd just been pillaged, and he was grinning all over his face as if he'd just got the OBE.

'I would have been in earlier,' he said, 'but what with the press and everything . . . . Oh, and the TV people are coming this afternoon.'

Now I began to see the picture. He was actually glad he'd been done because now he'd be a celebrity . . . but I only knew the half of it.

He put a cigarette in a long holder and sat back in the armchair. 'You know Sykes,' he said, 'the more I think about this burglary, the more I realize how carefully planned it was.'

I looked at Hat and winked, but she was so busy trying to look desirable that she missed it.

'Yes,' he went on. 'Three homes have been robbed in the street, and all of us top people . . . . He looked round for an ashtray and Hat jumped up and came towards him with cupped hands. He ignored her, and the ash fell on the floor. Hat went sheepishly back to her chair but I stared pointedly at the carpet. If it was me that had done that I wouldn't have heard the end of it . . . but then I'm not Mr Brown. If he came in with a dustbin and emptied it on the table Hat would say, 'Oh, thank you' . . . .

Anyway, Mr Brown went on: 'Oh, yes. These burglaries aren't haphazard you know. There's thought behind them.'

'Thought?' I said.

He stared at the ceiling . . . . 'Examine the facts. Three weeks ago they burgled two doors lower down. Then they go in next door. They miss you, of course . . . and last night they come into me. Do you see the point?'

Oh, I got the drift now all right. According to Mr Brown

being burgled was a status symbol. He wasn't getting away with that. I looked at him steadily: 'They'll probably come into us later on when they get the hang of it; they're probably working up to ours.'

His eyebrow lifted again. 'I hardly think they'll bother you, Sykes. This gang know where the good stuff is.'

Hat was hanging on his every word . . . . If she was invited to Buckingham Palace she'd tell the Queen she lived next door to Charles Brown. And that's another thing – he calls it Buck House and he refers to the Queen as Betty Windsor. Well, I mean, I run my household with a firm though benevolent hand, but Hat would never let me get away with that kind of irreverence . . . .

All the time I've been thinking this he was still going on: 'Oh yes, I'm well insured of course, so I shan't be out of pocket financially. It's the family heirlooms that can't be replaced.'

I got up and walked to the window. 'We've got property too, you know,' I said.

'Oh yes,' he replied, 'you've got a nice little cosy place here, a few sturdy bits of furniture. But really, Sykes, there's nothing here that would attract a top-class burglar.' He glanced round the room, then sauntered over to the wall: '. . . Unless of course your burglar is a pot duck fancier.' And he chortled.

Hat simpered happily. 'We bought those in Wimbledon,' she said.

He smirked. 'Very nice, too. I suppose they'll fetch about fifty pence in Shepherds Bush market.'

Hat straightened the little duck at the end. 'Oh, we weren't thinking of selling them,' she said.

Poor old Hat. She couldn't see that he was taking the micky, but I wasn't going to let him get away with it. 'They're not brilliant,' I said, 'but for your information they cost over a pound in 1947.' He looked at me pityingly, and I could feel myself getting uptight. I gestured towards the room in general: 'Oh yes, I agree it doesn't look much. As you say, a few sturdy bits of furniture – but that's deliberate.'

Mr Brown's eyes narrowed. 'What do you mean, *deliberate*?' he said.

'Ah! You're curious now, aren't you?'

'Not at all,' he said loftily. 'Just wondering what feeble excuse you're concocting for having to live here.'

I looked at him steadily. 'I'm not concocting excuses,' I said. 'I agree with you it does look cheap, ordinary, in fact downright suburban.' Hat was about to protest but I stopped her. 'Oh yes,' I said, 'but we don't have to live like this. We could have a big leather settee if we wanted, Persian rugs, a chandelier – we could have *four* ducks if we wanted – but we decided this was the clever way.' I tapped the side of my nose knowingly and winked.

'I'll go and put the kettle on for some tea,' said Hat, and went into the kitchen flashing me the 'why don't I shut up' look. And I would willingly have left it like that, with an air of mystery hanging about, but Mr Brown's a niggler.

'I fail to see how living in a slum condition can be deemed clever.'

I lit a cigarette with studied nonchalance. 'Let's put it this way,' I said. 'You wouldn't walk through the dock area at night carrying a jewel case, with a big gold chain round your neck.'

'What *are* you talking about?' he said.

I smiled at the end of my cigarette and said nothing. Hat came in with the tea things. 'Have the police any idea who did it?' she said. Mr Brown ignored her.

'What has walking round the docks in a gold chain got to do with my being robbed?' he said.

I took my tea from Hat, and said: 'Think about it.'

'Would you like a biscuit, Mr Brown?' gushed Hat.

'No, thank you,' he snapped, eyes never leaving me. His

composure was slipping and I was beginning to enjoy myself. 'Are you trying to tell me Sykes, that you deliberately live like this, so burglars will give you a miss?'

'Got it.' I said. 'Oh yes, a lot of people have access to houses – postmen, milkmen, gas meter men – and when they see your place, they go: "Hello, he's worth a bob or two." ' Mr Brown sniffed in derision, but I pressed on. 'I'm not saying they've got anything to do with the burglaries, but people do talk, and there's a lot of big ears about. Now the gas meter man, the coalman, they come in here and the first thing they do is go "Pooh!" '

Hat slammed her cup down in her saucer. Mr Brown snorted derisively: 'I see now all this is just a blind. Your heirlooms are tucked away somewhere safe – silver plate, jewellery, priceless antiques.' He chortled again.

I put down my cup and saucer deliberately and stared at Hat. 'Have you been talking?' I said. She looked back at me in astonishment.

Mr Brown downed his tea and stood up. 'You know, Sykes, you really are pathetic. "Priceless family heirlooms".'

I stubbed out my cigarette. 'I'd rather we didn't say any more about it.'

'I'm sure you wouldn't,' he crowed, 'because you haven't got any.'

Now if there's one thing that gets me going it's being crowed at, especially by Mr Brown. Caution went out of the window. 'Oh, haven't we?' I said. 'You're not the only one who's been bequeathed, you know. We have more family heirlooms in that strong box than you've had hot dinners.'

'What strong box?' he said.

'In the cellar.'

Hat looked at the ceiling in exasperation and I knew I'd gone too far, but Mr Brown affects me like a match in a fireworks factory. He straightened his tie and his eyes were crafty. 'I'd like to see these fabulous heirlooms,' he purred.

'Well you can't,' I snapped, 'because we keep the keys at the bank.' Hat was now behind Mr Brown, giving me 'I'll murder you' over his shoulder, but that sort of threat only makes me more reckless. 'And what's more,' I said, 'the box is not allowed to be opened except in the presence of two solicitors.' A nice authentic touch, I thought.

Mr Brown's composure was slipping. He'd strolled in here full of condescension to remind the peasants why they were peasants and why he was the squire, and here he was with all the bounce knocked out of him. He really is no match for me. He tried to pull himself together. 'Well, if you've got all these things, Sykes, it seems rather strange that you haven't been burgled yet.'

'It's not strange at all,' I said. 'They'd like to. . . . Oh yes, this is the big one all right. They'd *like* to very much, but they wouldn't dare.'

'Why wouldn't they dare?' he said, suspiciously.

By now my imagination was way ahead of my tongue, and I was almost believing it all myself. Indeed I'd made a mental note to have the box moved to the vaults of the bank . . . and then I realized there wasn't a box. 'I'll tell you why they wouldn't dare – because of Nero.'

'Nero,' he said, and looked quickly at Hat. She wasn't any help. She was pretending to wind up the cuckoo clock, but I could tell by the expression on her back that as soon as Mr Brown had gone I was in for a real ding-dong.

'Yes, Nero.' I repeated. 'My dog, specially trained for us by the police. That's the reason we haven't been burgled.'

'Really, Sykes,' he said, all silky, 'I'd very much like to see this dog of yours, or are you only allowed to show him in the presence of two solicitors?' He chuckled at Hat and she smiled a sickly smile back.

I realized that he was gaining the ascendancy again, so I played it cool: 'You can't see him today because he's down at the police dog school; and when he comes back he gets his food, then he's on guard again.'

'But don't you ever let him out?' he said.

'I daren't. I had to promise the police that I wouldn't. He's too ferocious.'

Mr Brown looked at me suspiciously. 'But surely, Sykes . . . I'd have heard him bark?'

'Bark?' I said. 'I won't let him. That's why he's such a good guard dog. You should see him every night checking all the doors – it's uncanny. I tell you I wouldn't like to be the one to break into here at night.'

He looked at me steadily. 'Quite frankly,' he said, making his way to the door, 'I don't believe a word of it, but I'll be round tomorrow to see this wonder dog of yours.' And with that he went.

As the door closed Hat exploded. 'Well, you've done it now, haven't you? You've really gone over the top this time.'

'For goodness sake don't you start,' I said, and turned away.

She was round the front of me like a shot. 'Go on. Tell me why you always have to tell such lies all the time. Go on. Why?'

'Why?' I said. 'I'll tell you why. I did it for you, that's why.'

She was amazed.

'Oh yes,' I went on. 'I deliberately try to shield you and this is all the thanks I get.'

Her mouth kept opening but her brain couldn't find the words.

'Listen, Hat,' I said, getting her to sit down. 'Do you want to walk down the street and have everybody pointing at you, and looking at you with pity, because you're too poor to be burgled? Is that what you want? You know what will happen. Letters will start coming in with the odd pound note. Food parcels will be left on the doorstep.

People will stop you at the market and slip an odd frock or two in your basket. Do you want the welfare people round twice a week?' She was calmer now, feeling a bit sorry for herself, and I could almost hear the violins in the background. . . . 'You heard what Mr Brown said, "There's nothing here worth pinching" . . . I don't want people thinking we're not as good as he is because we haven't been burgled.'

She pulled herself out of her reverie. 'You're right, Eric,' she said. 'The only thing is you'll have to get a dog.'

That floored me. Come what might there wasn't going to be a dog in this house. Dogs and me are natural enemies. They all go for me – even one that was tranquillized and had no teeth would try and bowl me over. 'No fear, Hat. We're not getting a dog.'

'But you'll have to now, after what you told Mr Brown . . . and it'll have to be a big one.'

'No dog,' I said.

'All right,' she said. 'If you don't mind losing face.'

I came back fast. 'It's not a question of losing face,' I said. 'It's limbs – arms, legs . . . *bits*.'

She went off into the kitchen and I sat there and pondered what to do. I could put a black armband on and say that the dog had been killed crossing the road, but that's no good – knowing Mr Brown he'd insist on seeing the remains. Or I could go round the streets whistling for a day or two, saying it was lost. Anyway I decided to sleep on it. I often to go bed when I have a problem. Once I didn't get up for a week and I still hadn't solved the problem. As a matter of fact I'd forgotten what it was – which is the next best thing.

It was the middle of the following morning. I was propped up in bed, wondering whether I should ring down for another egg, when the idea hit me like an exploding star-shell. In two shakes of a duck's tail I was dressed. I must have knocked seconds off my other quick dressing time, only on this occasion I ran down my own stairs instead of having to drop out of a first-floor window. That's the worst of the night shifts these days; you never know when they're going to come out on strike.

Anyway, when I got downstairs Hat shouted from the kitchen: 'Oh, you're up then.'

'Yes,' I said. Then I put on my coat and let myself out. All the time Hat was talking to me from the kitchen. I could still hear her when I turned the corner of the street. . . .

In an hour I was back, and as I hung up my coat Hat came out of the kitchen, still talking. 'Well,' she said. 'What d'you think, then?'

'I said it's a marvellous idea,' I said, and she went back into the kitchen quite happy. I wondered what I'd agreed to. I don't suppose I'll ever know now. Anyway I had a big surprise for her, which I set up, then I slipped into the kitchen. 'Listen to this, Hat,' I said.

She cocked her head on one side. 'What?' she said.

'Shhh. . . . Listen!' And we waited for a few seconds. Then *woof woof*, a colossal great dog bark. . . .

Hat's face lit up. 'Oh, let me see him,' and she rushed into the living-room. She looked behind the settee and up the staircase, and the dog still barked away. 'Come on, Eric,' she said, 'where is he?'

'You're leaning on him,' I said, and she sprang back. I lifted the lid of the gramophone.

'It's a record,' she said.

'Yes.' How's that for quick thinking? 'Now Mr Brown can hear Nero barking, and we don't have any hassles. No licence necessary, we don't have to feed him, and he's house-trained.'

'You'll never get away with it,' she said.

'Oh, no? It fooled you, didn't it?' which she grudingly admitted.

A prophet is without honour in his own country. . . . I mean why can't she come straight out and say I'm a genius?

If Mr Brown had thought of a trick like that she'd be writing off about it to the newspapers. . . . Never mind about that, though, there was plenty to do yet before I was finished. I got one of my old leather belts and put studs in it. Hat was mystified.

'It's his collar,' I said.

She laughed, but I could see she was entering into the conspiracy. When she came back from shopping she had something wrapped in a newspaper.

'What you got there?' I said.

She unwrapped it. 'It's Nero's dinner. It's a hambone,' she said. And what a size – it looked to me more like the thigh of a Suffolk Punch.

And then again, another of those flashes of brilliance . . . I found an old tin bath in the cellar, put a bit of water in it and wrote 'Nero' on the side.

The scene was set. All I had to do now was bring on the sucker. I couldn't wait to see Mr Brown's face when he saw all the paraphernalia. The gramophone would be going full blast in the kitchen, with me keeping guard with a chair in one hand and a bull whip in the other. The minute I rang the doorbell that evening I briefed Hat on what she had to do. Having done so, I put a fresh needle in the gramophone, wound it up, and showed her the exact spot on the record to get the maximum effect. Then I set off for the station to meet Mr Brown – accidentally, of course – on his way home. Bang on time there he was, showing his season ticket at the barrier, smiling all over his face and turning from side to side so they could all get a good look at him . . . and he'd only been on television for two minutes. I fell into step beside him.

'I thought it was you,' I said.

'Ah, Sykes,' he beamed. 'How's that dog of yours getting on?'

'All right,' I said, non-committally. 'It looks like we'll be having some rain.'

'I must say, Sykes, you keep him awfully quiet. I strolled round the back of your house last night and didn't hear a sound.'

'Oh, never mind about Nero,' I said. I was stringing him along beautifully. 'That's a nice briefcase you've got there', I said, as if trying to change the subject.

'Is he at home yet, or is he still at the police school?'

'Oh, he's at home. He only goes to the school twice a week.'

'Not studying for his O levels then, is he?' And he chuckled. He never laughs really, he always chuckles. Hat thinks it's infectious, but I think he's wary about his teeth coming out. 'Do you know what, Sykes?' he said. 'I think I'll pop in as I go by and say hello to your Nero.'

I pretended to be flustered. 'Oh no, I wouldn't do that,' I said. 'He's been in a bad temper today. I don't think that horse's head agreed with him.'

By this time we were at our gate, and I acted as if I didn't want him to get by. I only hoped Hat wouldn't panic and put the wrong record on. It'd be just like her to do that, so that when I shouted through the letter box 'Down, Nero' we'd hear 'A Sleepy Lagoon' by Mantovani. Mr Brown brushed by me and rang the doorbell. Straightaway there was a great bark. Well, he sprang back from that doorbell as if it had ten thousand volts coming through it.

I looked at him ruefully. 'I told you, didn't I?' Then I shouted: 'Down, Nero. Down, boy . . . the master's home.' I must say Hat was doing a great job. She was obviously moving about the room with the gramophone in her arms and every so often she'd lurch against the door as if Nero was trying to get out. 'We're going in now,' I said to Mr Brown. 'Don't show fear. Give me your bowler hat so he can get a sniff of it, but don't show fear. They can smell when ——.' But I never finished what I was going to say because when I looked round he'd vanished; his briefcase was on the path and there was still a faint whiff of brilliantine in the air. I mean, he really shouldn't tangle with me; he's out of his depth, I thought, as I let myself in. 'I'm home, Hat,' I said automatically. 'It sounded great, Hat. I . . .' And as I turned from the coat rack an enormous black dog leapt at me and bashed me against the staircase. 'Hat!' I shouted. 'Hat!'

By this time the dog had hold of the back of my jacket and was dragging me into the kitchen, with me like a fool saying, 'Good dog, good dog.' I grabbed hold of a chair to save myself, but all that happened was that me and the chair ended up by the fridge. Then the dog backed off, no doubt to select which piece he'd have first. What a monster! I'd never seen anything like it – he must have been a cross between a Dobermann and a mastiff, but part panther. He was crouched ready to spring and I edged slowly along the floor toward the kitchen door . . . then, all slavering jaws and teeth, he sprang, and with a tremendous yelp I rolled to one side. Bang! He hit the fridge with such a crash that I heard the milk bottle breaking insde, and the door flew open. That was the only thing that saved me. Sunday's joint fell out and the dog spotted it – that dog was no fool; he knew the meat might go off, but I'd keep for another day, so he got stuck into the joint. Gradually I eased towards the back door and opened it gently. Now I had to do the tricky part . . . while he was crunching on a piece I kicked the rest of it outside. In a flash he was after it and I slammed the door, shot the bolts and slumped back against it in a trembling mass of humanity. After a time I took stock of myself and found I was all there, but the back of my jacket had gone. I was still standing by the door, white-faced, when Hat poked her head in.

'What's all the noise about?' she said, as if nothing had happened. 'I must have been upstairs when you came in.'

I tried to speak, but my throat had dried up.

'Did you say hello to Rex?' she said.

I wiped the sweat off me. 'Rex', I croaked. 'Where did you get that thing from?'

She said: 'It's really funny. Just after you'd gone this man came to the door. He was a detective or something, and asked me a lot of questions about the burglaries, and did I live alone, you know, all that sort of thing . . . and did we have anything of value . . . he knows Madge – and Oooh,' she said, 'and you know Madge went to the doctor's with her leg' – I stopped her quickly.

'I don't care if Madge went to the doctor's with both her legs. I want to know about that dog.' Hat was a bit put out, but she does go on once she gets started, and to tell you the truth I'm up to here with Madge and her surgical stocking. 'The dog,' I said. 'How did you come across that werewolf?'

She said, 'Oh, Rex. Well this man had Rex with him, he is a police dog by the way, and apparently he's been with the drug squad, and he's got four sons.' . . . I realized it was the detective who had the family, not the dog, but I'd had all the fight knocked out of me so I just had to let her go on . . . eventually after the eldest boy was twelve and was going to be a jockey and you wouldn't think he had a wig on . . . the detective, not the aspiring jockey . . . it was ten minutes later before she got round to the information I was after. Apparently the detective was going to be in the district making enquiries, and Hat had agreed to look after the dog for a few days. 'By the way,' she said, 'where is he?'

'Where is he? I'll tell you where. He's out there terrorizing the countryside. There'll be panic in the streets, dead cattle all over the place. They'll have to call the army in.'

'He was only playing with you,' said Hat.

'Playing! Yes, I've seen a lion playing with a gazelle, but only when it's had enough to eat. . . . By the way,' I went on, 'we'll be having egg and chips for Sunday lunch.'

Hat stopped and listened. . . . 'What's that?' she said.

Then she went through to the living-room and I heard her open the front door. A stab of panic gripped me. I heard her say: 'Ooo's a naughty boy then,' and I knew it wasn't Mr Brown at the door. I was struggling to pull the fridge in front of the kitchen door when Hat popped her head in 'Come and say hello to Rex,' she said. 'He's come back.'

'I'm not saying hello to that thing,' I said. My voice didn't sound like mine but I wasn't going to introduce myself again. I know they do marvellous things with artificial limbs, but I'm too old now to start that game. No. I was resolved to sleep in the kitchen, or better still sneak out the back way and get a hotel room somewhere.

Half an hour later, Hat popped her head through the serving hatch. 'It's all right,' she said, 'he's asleep.'

Suppose he's pretending.' I said.

'No, look. He's stretched out on the settee.'

I poked my head round the door, and sure enough there he was on the settee, and stretched out was the right expression. It's a big settee but his head was flopping over one arm, and his back legs were on the table by the window. I knew now that my bedroom was the safest place. I could barricade the door and even the incredible hulk wouldn't be able to leap up through the window. So gradually, moving sideways and using Hat for a shield, I made my way upstairs. In the last couple of yards to sanctuary I panicked, and rushed in pulling Hat with me. I was only just in time, for as I slammed the door that dog was off the settee and up the stairs in two strides, and the door shuddered as he flung himself at it. Me and Hat were struggling to get a chest of drawers in front of it. He had another leap at the door and a panel splintered, but by the time he'd gathered himself for another go, the drawers were firmly in place, with my bed wedged in front of them, and me and Hat sitting on it for extra protection.

Hat looked at me, frightened. 'He's been quiet all the

afternoon,' she said. She tried to talk to it through the crack in the door, but it snarled and had another go, and so it went on. That was the longest night I've ever spent. I only managed a few hours' sleep while Hat kept watch. Well, after all, it was Hat who brought the dog in in the first place, and it was my bedroom.

When I opened my eyes it was light, and Hat was dozing in a chair with a blanket round her shoulders. It was my thick blanket, too – no wonder I never got warm. I knelt quietly up in bed, and put my eye to the crack, but I couldn't see the dog. Then I whispered, 'Rex . . . Rex, here boy,' but there was nothing.

Hat came up beside me. 'He's not there,' she said, and after ten minutes we decided that he must have gone, because no dog would have put up with some of the things I called him through that door. Very carefully we took down the barricades and Hat went out on the landing. Then she cautiously went downstairs. At the bottom she stopped abruptly.

I looked around my bedroom door: 'What's happening?' I whispered.

Hat looked back. 'Come down here and see for yourself,' she said.

When I looked round the room I couldn't take it in at first . . . the settee had gone, there was no carpet . . . no telly . . . it seems the only thing that was left was the goldfish bowl and the three pot ducks. Then the penny dropped. We turned to each other and both together we said: 'We've been burgled?' More importantly, they'd taken the dog as well. I know it seems funny now, but we were like a couple of kids on Christmas morning, dancing round as if Mafeking had been relieved again. Then the doorbell rang.

It was a police constable. 'Good morning, madam,' he said, and cleared his throat. 'As you know, there have been a series of burglaries in this area, and it is my duty to warn you of the method they may adopt.' We just stood and grinned at him – he must have thought we were mentally retarded so he hurried up with his duty. 'One of the gang may visit you posing as a detective. He arrives with a large black dog. He arranges to leave the aforesaid animal in order to lull the householder into a false sense of security, but later that evening the gang will arrive and ransack the house while the dog takes care of the occupants.' We were still grinning. 'I know, sir, that you may find this very hard to believe, but I can assure you. . . .' He stopped as I gestured grandly at the empty room. He pushed back his helmet: 'It's happened, hasn't it sir?'

I nodded and he took out his notebook.

At that moment Mr Brown strode in: 'Sykes,' he started, 'I really must complain about the noise last night and I. . . . .' He looked at the policeman, then at me and Hat; then he took in the room.

Hat said: 'Look, Mr Brown. We've been burgled.' She was beaming like an African sunrise.

He was astounded. 'You?' he said.

'Yes, *us*, Mr Brown,' I said triumphantly. 'Cleaned out . . . right out. Oh yes, they know where the stuff is all right. That makes four of us in this district. All top people . . . but they had to use a dog in ours.'

Mr Brown's shoulders sagged. He accepted defeat gracefully I'll say that for him. 'Ah well,' he said, 'let me give you a piece of advice from personal experience. Get on to your insurance people immediately.'

I looked at him blankly. 'Pardon.' I said in a small voice. He looked at me. 'The people you insured the stuff with.'

All the bubble went out of the day. Hat looked at me and I looked at Hat, and Mr Brown saw the look on our faces and started to laugh. And this time it wasn't a chuckle. We heard him laughing all the way to his house, supercilious old fool.

'I don't mind him being a vicar, but why does he go to church all the time?'

THE VICAR

Hat and I have an ideal set-up; being brother and sister we can come and go as we please, no strings, no ties, free as the air. As long as my meals are ready on time and the beds made every day what more can a man want? I've had a few girlfriends and Hat's stuck on Mr Brown, but there's no danger there because he'd never marry a commoner. So life is set fair with a following wind, or it was until a cloud no bigger than a hand appeared in the infinite blue. It was the new vicar, the Reverend Bentwell. In the normal course of events we would never have met him because we are not avid churchgoers. Well, the last time we went was over a year ago, when a rumour got round that the television people were coming to do *Songs of Praise*. Of course the church was packed, and Hat and me had to sit near the back, so we missed all the visual bits. In any case the TV people didn't turn up, so it didn't really matter, but what stuck in my gullet was all those people. I can remember mentioning it to Hat on the way home.

'Oh come on, Eric,' she said, 'you're not a regular. The last time you went was the thanksgiving service for the end of the war.'

'I'm not talking about that. What bugs me is half those people weren't even Church of England.'

'How d'you know?' she said.

'Because a lot of them came in and genuflected.'

She stopped and looked over her shoulder to see if I'd been overheard. 'They did what?' she said.

I repeated every syllable slowly. 'Ge-nu-flect. And you don't have to genuflect if you're C of E.'

She looked at me in bewilderment: 'What do you mean, genuflect?'

I thrust my hands in my pockets in exasperation. 'Genuflect, woman,' I shouted. 'You know, ace, king, queen, jack,' and I did it for her.

'Oh yes,' she replied as the penny dropped. 'I saw one or two of them doing that.'

'Right,' I said. 'They're not our lot, they were just in there to get on telly.'

Hat nodded in agreement. 'We're the mugs, Hat. We're the members but we let anybody come in. I'll bet it'd be a different story if we tried to walk into their synagogue.'

. . . However, to get back to my story, during his first week of office the Reverend Bentwell came to visit us. It was a bright, sunny morning so I was up and about well before eleven o'clock when the doorbell rang. I was in the kitchen at the time trying to get egg off my dressing-gown. Hat popped her head in and said 'It's the new vicar,' but she said it in a way that meant 'for God's sake don't let him see you like that', so I stayed in the kitchen and tried to hear what was going on. I didn't get much, just the odd word and Hat's laugh – not the laugh when I tell her a joke but that twinkly sort she imagines is infectious. Anyway he didn't stay long, but after he'd gone Hat was a changed woman. She didn't even give me a rocket for looking like a tramp in the out-patient's department; she just sat there.

'What did he want?' I said.

She dragged her gaze away from nothing. 'Who?'

'The vicar.'

She got up to go into the kitchen, saying: 'This isn't getting the dinner ready, is it?'

I followed her. 'Is he married?'

'Married? I couldn't ask him that, could I?' she said.

But I knew she was gone, that whatever had passed between them had had a profound effect – she was standing at the sink peeling the soap. I wasn't unduly perturbed; she'd had those sudden crushes before and something always happened in time to prevent a permanent relationship. In a couple of days she'd be back to normal, asking Mr Brown if he wanted any shopping done and laughing at my vicar jokes. But it didn't work out like that.

The next Sunday she went to church – not just once, but matins *and* evensong. Then she went the next Sunday and the Sunday after that. So the following week I went with her just to see how things were going and I was flummoxed: what did she see in him? I didn't expect a Bing Crosby in *Going My Way* or even Barry Fitzgerald, but this one looked a bit of a nana. He was a tall, pale man who looked as if a good Yorkshire pudding wouldn't do him any harm – but then again that's the kind of person who always appeals to Hat's maternal instincts.

As I sat through his sermon I realized he was never going to make archbishop. First of all I couldn't catch half of what he said, and second there was only me and Hat in the congregation, so he wasn't a crowd-puller. Why he climbed into the pulpit and shouted I don't know; it would have been much easier for him to sit next to us and say, 'Now listen.'

Nevertheless, that was another danger. If I hadn't been present there would only have been him and Hat, so afterwards I had to go with her as a sort of chaperone. Hat was totally besotted by him: when he said 'Let us pray' Hat was down like a shot, not just leaning forward but actually on her knees. Yes and she doesn't even do that when she's cleaning the fireplace. To his credit he never seemed to encourage her. The only contact they had as far as I could make out was at the end of the service when he walked up the aisle to the main door and waited for us to come out. Then he'd shake hands with me and Hat would drop a little curtsey; it was embarrassing really – the first time she did it I thought she was going to kiss his hand, and she wasn't far off.

I didn't really mind the going to church bit, because after all there was nothing much on telly at that time except *Stars on Sunday* and *Songs of Praise*, so it was better really to go out and see it live. However, at home things were getting a bit strained. I mean, religion's all right for Sunday, but you don't want it for the rest of the week unless you're a monk, in which case it's your living; but Hat really went in at the deep end – we had to have grace before every meal and its very frustrating having to bow your head when you're trying to watch television. During the evenings Hat would be embroidering a hassock or trying to memorize the hymns so she wouldn't have to take her eyes off the vicar. Then she took to popping into the church during the week with fresh flowers and polishing the artifacts and once when I was passing on the way to the Dog and Partridge she was sweeping round the gravestones.

I never tried to stand in her way as I may have done in the past – for her own protection, mind you. Never once did I visit the vicar on the quiet and put the spoke in, and apart from slipping a bottle of gin in the pew where Hat had been sitting I never did anything to discourage him. Nevertheless the affair didn't seem to be dying a natural death and I knew things would have to come to a head pretty soon. I was right.

One Sunday we'd just got back from the church – it was either Pentecost or Epiphany. I knew it was something important because Hat had put a pound note in the collection and I couldn't do much about it because I do the collections, and as there was only Hat and myself to return with an empty box would have looked a bit suspicious.

Anyway, over the last few weeks I'd made a bit of a profit, so I wasn't too upset, but when we got home I sensed a difference in the atmosphere. Normally I take my shoes and tie off and switch on the telly, while Hat goes into the kitchen to start the supper. This time she didn't; she sat down without even taking her hat off. Then she did something even more unprecedented – she got up and switched the telly off. Well, I mean nobody switches that set off except for me. We both have our various jobs to do around the house and switching the set on and off is mine. I considered for a moment just getting up and switching it on again, but Hat was standing right in front of it and it's a foolish man who tries to shift my sister when she has that look in her eye. So I gave her my exasperated expression and just waited.

'Eric,' she said, and I could see she was struggling for words. 'Eric, if I went, could you manage?'

'Manage?' I said. 'Of course I can manage. I'm not a geriatric. I don't mind you going off, as long as you're back by ten o'clock.'

'No, Eric. I mean if I got married.'

'Married.' I sat bolt upright.

'What do you mean "married". Has the vicar said anything?'

'No, well not in so many words, but tonight during the sermon I felt he was – well, he was reaching out to me.'

I had a sudden vision of the vicar in the pulpit reaching out to her and falling over the top, flat on his face. 'What do you mean, "reaching out"?'

'Well,' she said. 'His sermon tonight, the text was "Man cannot live by bread alone", and all the time he was speaking he was looking straight at me.'

I relaxed again. After all, the vicar had to look at somebody and there was only me and Hat, so she was just making a mountain out of a molehill. 'A sermon about "man cannot live on bread alone" isn't a proposal of marriage, you know,' I said.

'Eric, that poor man lives by himself at the vicarage. He doesn't even have a housekeeper, so when did he have a decent meal? He needs somebody, Eric, and – well, he can't come right out with it, being a vicar and everything, so it's up to me.'

I was astonished. 'You're not going to ask him for his hand, are you?'

'Of course I'm not, but tomorrow I thought I'd go down to the vicarage with a basket of food and cook him a really nice hot dinner – just say it's in appreciation for his good works and stuff. What do you think?'

I must admit I didn't like the idea at all. I mean the vicar might not reciprocate her feelings at the moment, but after he had had a bellyfull of Hat's roast beef and stuff he might find it hard to resist. However I could see she had made up her mind to go, so I magnanimously gave my consent.

'Thank you, Eric,' she said, and went happily into the kitchen.

After all, I'm not against Hat getting married as long as it's the right man and the vicarage was big enough for all of us. I'd never actually been inside the vicarage but it looked marvellous from the outside, lovely garden and probably large rooms. It might be a good idea to get a billard table in. I was so engrossed in my thoughts that I almost forgot to switch the set on again. During the night I gave the matter a little more thought and by morning I was almost looking forward to having a vicar in the family. It's a step up in society and I could invite the captain of the golf club round for tea on the vicarage lawn. After a quick game of croquet my application would be a mere formality.

There was a holiday atmosphere as I helped her pack her basket with a pot roast, some asparagus, and even a bottle of Beaujolais – the thought of it all made my mouth water, but Hat soon quashed my suggestion that I should go with her and she went off humming 'Rock of Ages'. When she'd gone I'd got busy with a tentative enquiry – a phone call to an estate agent. The news on the value of our house wasn't good: he said he knew of the property and thought it had been condemned; but with regard to my next question the vicarage was obviously worth a bob or two and why was I enquiring? I was non-commital and put the phone down. The next step would be to get the vicar to put it in his wife's name – a very straightforward tax dodge, and of course his wife being Hat she'd have to make a will.

Anyway I didn't think any further than that because the front door burst open as if it had been caught in the blast of a landmine and Hat burst in. She dumped her basket on the table, threw her hat at the cuckoo clock and stormed into the kitchen. I peeped into the basket, which still contained undisturbed beef, asparagus and Beaujolais; then I eased open the kitchen door to see what was happening, but Hat was busy getting the tea ready so I silently withdrew. I never interfere when she's in the middle of cooking. Once we're stuck into the eggs and bacon and the first pangs have been mollified that's the time to broach a subject.

In due course we sat down for tea. I bowed my head for grace but nothing happened, and when I looked up again she'd finished hers. By the time I got to mopping my plate with a piece of bread she'd already unpacked the basket, taken the hymn books up to the attic, had a couple of gins and had gone to bed. So I knew something traumatic had happened. It was four days later at bingo when I got the story out of her. She'd just had a housy-housy call and was in a good mood, so I casually said: 'How did it go the other day?' and it all poured out. Firstly she's never going to that church again, secondly she's in two minds whether to embrace the Moslem faith, and most important she's very ashamed of even contemplating leaving me on my own, so it all turned out well. I fell on my feet once again.

Incidentally what had happened was that she'd bowled up to the vicarage all happy and full of the joys of living, ready to prepare a cosy five-star meal for two. She rang the doorbell of the vicarage, the door swung open, and who should answer but the organist in a little frilly apron with a feather-duster in his hand.

THE END IS NIGH

'If you really thought the world was going to end, you'd have your hair done.'

My sister Hat is the most gullible person I know; it's pathetic – she'll believe anybody unless it's me. For instance if Mr Brown walked in in the middle of July and said 'It's snowing,' she'd immediately light the fire. But if I walked in wet through and said 'It's raining,' she'd go to the door and hold her hand out. She's the same with television adverts; whatever it is, she'll go straight out and buy it. Washing powder, polish, chocolates, we've even got a dozen tins of Pal meat with nutritious bonemeal, although we've never had a dog of our own and as long as I'm in charge we're never likely to have one. However, it was all fairly harmless until the other day. . . .

A man was walking down the street with a sandwich board which said 'THE END IS NIGH'. Straightaway Hat stops the milk. Well, I mean this was ridiculous and I told her so. I had to shout because she was lighting a Hamlet cigar at the time. That's another thing – she never smoked before she saw the advert on telly; now she not only gets through ten a day but she's bought a record to go with it. She sits back, lights up, then sets the music going. That's why I had to shout.

'Listen, Hat,' I started. . . . It was no good – she was in another world, so I switched off the gramophone and tried again. She didn't pay any attention. She looked at her watch and turned on the television in case they were advertising something she'd missed. I switched that off as well. She stared at me as if I'd just thrown an egg at the Queen's portrait.

'Now listen, Hat,' I said. 'You're susceptible, you mustn't believe everything anybody says.'

'What d'you mean?' she replied in all innocence.

'You know what I mean, that bloke walking about with the 'END IS NIGH' board.'

'It's not just him,' she said. 'The end *is* nigh.'

'OK, OK. The end is nigh. When's it going to be?'

She looked at me, then walked to the window. . . 'Tomorrow night.'

I was flabbergasted. I mean, she comes out with some stupid things sometimes, but she's never really dogmatic about them. 'Tomorrow night?'

'Yes,' she said, 'and we're all going on to the top of Knockers Hill.'

'Oh, are we?' I said. 'Well, I'm not going to spend tomorrow night on Knockers Hill, that's for sure.'

She looked at me with that expression she uses on Mr Brown when she's trying to get him to eat another piece of her home-made pie.

'Please, Eric.'

'Look, Hat,' I said. 'If it *is* the end of the world tomorrow, it will end whether we're on top of Knockers Hill freezing to death or sitting here by the fire watching *Blue Peter*.'

'Everybody round here's going,' she said.

'Well that's nothing, is it? . . . Get a couple of sheepdogs and you can move this lot anywhere.' I switched on the television again, but Hat switched it off.

'All right,' I said. 'What's so special about being at the top of Knockers Hill?'

'Ah, yes,' she said. 'Why did Noah go to the top of Mount Ararat?'

'What's Noah got to do with it?' I said. 'In any case, he built a boat up there, and you haven't left me a lot of time.'

It was then I noticed a half-packed suitcase on the chair in the corner, and I realized she was serious. I walked over and picked through the contents. It was ridiculous the stuff she was taking; I mean, for one's last night on earth it would be reasonable to take the Bible, a hymn book or the dialogues of Plato, but all she'd packed was Scrabble. I held it up with a questioning look.

'Oh, well,' she said. 'You like Scrabble and it'll help pass the time.'

I tried another approach. 'Come on, Hat, you don't really believe it's going to be the end of the world, do you?'

'Yes, I do,' she said, 'and it's not just me – look at the paper.' She picked up the *Daily Express* and held it in front of my face. 'Read that,' she said. 'Panic in America, general exodus to Mount Vernon, all roads to Mount Vernon blocked. . . .'

I stopped her before she could read the whole bit. 'I know all that,' I said. 'I've read it too.'

'Oh no, you haven't,' she said, 'you only read the football.'

'All right, all right, so all roads to Mount Vernon are blocked. I'll bet they are. . . . I'll bet there are private coaches hired for hundreds of dollars a seat, popcorn stands, jumbo jets cruising at thirty thousand feet full of vicars so when the end comes they can be first in.' Hat's eyes glazed, so I knew she was getting the picture. I pressed on: 'That's America, Hat – can you imagine it? Television cameras and a man with a bow tie. Hello folks, here we are on Mount Vernon. In a few moments from now, exclusively on NBC, we bring you the end of the world. But first do you suffer from backache, stiffness or painful haemorrhoids? If so get Magirub, the great little ointment from your friendly downtown drugstore.'

Hat looked at me steadily. 'You always have to mock everything, don't you?'

'No I don't, Hat, but only an idiot would spend a night up on Knockers Hill.'

'Really?' she said, one eyebrow going up. 'Well, Mr Finglebaum's going, and he's not an idiot, he's a big businessman.'

'Ah well,' I said. 'If he's going it's a tax dodge. Anyway, if you believe it's going to be the end of the world then go up on Knockers Hill, but I'm staying here.'

With that I sat down, picked up the paper and turned to the sports page. I pretended to read, hoping she'd go into the kitchen or dust a chair or something, but she just hovered there and I could sense we hadn't finished yet. I put the paper down. 'All right then, how's the world going to end? A big bang, rising flood water, a sign in the sky saying "Walk this way"?'

She took out a tiny hanky and dabbed her nose. 'I don't know how it will end,' she said. 'But please, Eric, please, if it does end, I want us to be together.'

I read the signs. Next thing she'd be in tears, then up to her room and lock the door, and I could miss a couple of meals, so I got up and patted her arm. 'Look Hat,' I said, rather like a doctor who's just taken your leg off by mistake, and is now explaining what good crutches they make these days. 'Look Hat, I'm only trying to be reasonable. It says end of the world in America, and it may well be true, but that doesn't mean to say it will happen here as well.'

She thought about it for a moment, then she said: 'It'll happen all over at the same time.'

'Will it?' I said.

'Well, it's all one world, isn't it?'

'Oh yes, it's all one world,' I said. 'I'm not disputing that. But what day is it today?'

'It's Tuesday.'

'Exactly. It's Tuesday. But if you got on the phone to America and said what day is it, they'd say Wednesday.'

She looked at me, perplexed: 'Why would they say that?'

'Because it's Wednesday over there. There's a time difference – they're twenty-four hours ahead of us, so the point I'm making is this – if it's the end of the world over there, and the people on Mount Vernon are saved, then by all means I'll go up with you to Knockers Hill.' She sat down slowly to digest this, but I didn't want her to examine it too closely so I rubbed my hands together vigorously and said: 'OK, now how about a spot of lunch?'

She didn't move, but just sat staring into space, and I could almost see her brain struggling to function.

'Shall I open a tin of Spam?' I said. I don't think she heard me.

'Yes, but according to the experts. . . .'

I was on to it right away. 'Experts?' I said. 'What experts? Madge? Mr Brown?'

'It's not just them. Last night on television, Patrick Moore said that there were disturbing signs in the sky.'

I was very hungry now and beginning to lose patience. 'Patrick Moore?' I shouted. 'Patrick Moore's an idiot, that's what he is. He went to the other side of the world to watch an eclipse. Twelve thousand miles to watch an eclipse – I saw it out of the back bedroom window.'

Hat sprang to his defence – she fancies him and would give her eye teeth just to press his suit. 'It wasn't the same one though, was it?'

'What do you mean, it wasn't the same one? There's only one sun and one moon, Hat. They don't have different ones all over the world.'

'All right,' she said. 'Why is it that in Africa their sun is hotter than ours?'

I was dumbfounded. There are times when I find it very hard to believe that we come from the same parents. 'Look, Hat,' I said, 'I haven't got time to go into a geophysical discussion. Let's have some lunch and then we'll. . . .'

'Never mind the lunch. Answer me that – why does Africa have a hotter sun than we do?'

'Why?' I said. 'Why? I'll tell you why. Africa is on the equator and the sun is hot but by the time it gets to us a lot of its heat has been used up.' She didn't appear to be convinced, so I went on. 'If you look out of the window every morning the sun comes up, doesn't it?'

'Yes,' she said. 'Go on.'

'All right, and its come up from the equator. This very fact means that is takes a lot of energy out of itself, so it's drained of heat, and it's cold in England, but when it starts to go down again at night making for the equator and because it's going downwards it's picking up heat again. That's why the sun is hotter in Africa.'

She looked at me with new respect.

'Now then, are there any more questions or can we think about lunch?'

She collected herself. 'It'll be some time,' she said, 'because I thought we'd have roast beef. Then I can make sandwiches for us to take up tomorrow night.'

'Oh, for goodness sake. You're not still on about Knockers Hill are you?'

'Oh Eric, please, it'll only be one night.'

I wasn't going to start all that again, especially as the thought of hot roast beef had started my gastric juices going.

'I'll think about it,' I said, and ushered her into the kitchen. No way was I going to spend a night on a cold hill.

However, and to my great astonishment, all the following day people were making their way past the house in the direction of Knockers Hill. Madge popped in with a bag of warm doughnuts and promised to bring some more when she went to await the end, and as I was looking out of the window a couple of dolly birds went past wearing T-shirts which said 'THE END IS NIGH'. It could be quite a ball up there, and I began to change my mind a little.

In any event later that evening Hat and I got off the bus at the end of Coopers Lane, and I was amazed – I'd expected to see one or two people making their way to the top of Knockers Hill, but this wasn't a handful of fanatics. This was a pilgrimage – whole families, couples, prams, dogs – all trudging upwards, and Knockers Hill itself was not a huge black pudding in the night – it was illuminated by a hundred bonfires as if this hill had been the target for an incendiary bombing raid. Suppose all these people were right after all, and I was wrong. Perhaps tonight *was* our last. I experienced a sudden tightening of the bowels, and I wished I'd gone before I came out.

I hurried on to catch up with Hat, who was slightly ahead of me. She was beginning to puff a bit now – the hill wasn't too steep but there was a lot of it. I watched her struggle under the weight of an enormous load of possessions; had she been a mule the RSPCA would have arrested me on the spot. As she paused for breath I felt a wave of affection and hurried forward to take one of the smaller suitcases from her.

It was hard to define the atomsphere – it wasn't gloomy or tearful, nor was it festive. It was just a gathering. Over by a clump of bushes a Salvation Army band was playing. The bandmaster, tall and cadavrous, was conducting vigorously – more for warmth than tempo. He turned in my direction and I saw he had two large lumps of cotton wool stuck in his ears in order to muffle the shrieks and clatter and the tinny background of countless transistor radios (or perhaps he just hated 'Onward Christian Soldiers'). There were a couple of coffee stalls, and an ambulance, and as we moved to higher ground a bookie had set up shop. Honest Fred, the punter's friend, was offering ten thousand to one against it being the end of the world before dawn, and such was the gullibility of people that he was doing a roaring trade. I mean, couldn't they see that if the world did end, Honest Fred wouldn't be there to pay out, and even worse they wouldn't be there to collect. However ten thousand to one isn't a bad bet so I had a fiver just in case. Then I trudged on.

Mercifully Hat stopped, having found her territory, and shed her load. Thankfully I sat down on one of her suitcases while she set about putting up the windbreak we had bought for the beach in Worthing. Down below I could see the lights twinkling, and the thought passed through my mind what a carnival night it would be for burglars. The man with the sandwich board stating, 'THE END IS NIGH' could be the burglar, and here was a carefully thought-out scheme to clear the town, but then I remembered I'd seen him on the flat just below the hill directing motorists into a makeshift car park. He had a peaked cap on, and the bag around his neck appeared to be somewhat weighty. He at least understood human frailties. By now the windbreak was up and we had some protection from the biting north-east wind; I was almost cosy – well, I would be when Hat had finished getting the fire going.

Deep down I didn't really believe it was going to be the end of the world, but around me there were people who apparently didn't share my view. Over by the fire on our left an old lady was having hysterics; she must have been over eighty, so a couple of days either way wouldn't have made much difference, but it turned out it wasn't to do with the world ending. A spark had set her frock alight. There was a slight thump on the back of the windbreak and I looked over the top. It was Mr Mardington rolling and grappling about with a young woman, who said 'Give over, Wilfred,' but she never slackened her grip on him. She must have seen the dark blob of my head above the windbreak, because she struggled up and helped Mr Mardington to his feet, and they hurried off into the night. Incidentally later on I saw Mrs Mardington sitting very close to the gasman, spoonfeeding him from a can of beans.

Hat was now bending over the basket and I was about to mention Mr Mardington, when I heard a couple of screams and turned just in time to see a streaker. He shot out of the gloom, leapt over one of the fires and veered towards us. As he passed he patted Hat on the backside and disappeared into the gloom again. He had a mask over his face so I didn't recognize him, but Hat said it was Norman Penderwell and continued rummaging in the basket. I could hardly believe it. Norman's such a quiet chap, and does odd jobs round the house when I'm at work.

Hat handed me a cup of soup and I was just blowing to cool it down when wallop, it was dashed from my lips and Madge fell on top of me. Madge runs the bread shop across the road and she's always fancied me. Well, twenty years ago she was a bit of a cracker, and had I not had a duty towards Hat, I might have thought seriously about her. However I'm glad I didn't now because she started to sag early. Well, I suppose making bread all your life you begin to look like a cottage loaf, and if it hadn't been for her doughnuts I would have terminated the relationship years ago. She still had a yen for me, though, but now here she was, arms around my neck, eyes staring at me like Pontefract cakes in a lump of suet.

'Hello, Madge,' I said, licking the soup off my hand.

'Say you love me, Ricky. Just once, before the end.'

'Madge,' I said, trying to ease away, 'it's not the end.'

Her face was an inch from mine, and I could smell the Guinness. 'Ricky, oh Ricky, just let me hear you say it once.'

I was trapped. If I said I loved her that would be the end of my freedom, and if I didn't she was strong enough to break my back. 'Madge,' I started, but before I could say anything else she was hauled off me – it was Nellie Limberk.

Madge swung round at her, 'What do you want?' she said.

Nellie ignored her and flung her arms round my neck.

Now I was really surprised. Nellie was a clippie on the number 28 bus, but apart from a bit of a badinage and the odd wink nothing had ever passed between us, and here she was, arms round me, planting great slurpy kisses all over my face. Madge dragged her off and gave me such a belt across my head I literally saw stars. I staggered back.

Nellie rounded on Madge and said, 'Go home, you silly cow.'

Madge lunged with her handbag, missed Nellie and caught me smack in the face again. Then she glared at Nellie and said: 'You can have him, he's useless, and tell him the next time he wants a doughnut from me I'll stuff it up his nose.' Then she ran away crying.

Nellie grabbed me again, and again she was hauled off, but this time he was a big, red-haired fellow. 'So this is him, is it?' he said and landed a clout right on the other side of my head, and that put my lights out for the next ten minutes. When I came to, Hat and the red-haired fellow were bending over me.

'Are you all right, Eric?' said Hat, wiping my head with a damp cloth. My ear was giving out a high-pitched howl and my lip felt like a hot water melon.

The red-haired man leaned over. 'I'm sorry, I shouldn't have done that,' he said.

I tried to speak but my mouth wouldn't obey my brain.

'This is Kenneth,' said Hat. 'Nellie's brother.'

'Yes,' he said. 'She's gone mad tonight, you're the fourth fellow she's been with.'

'That's OK,' I managed to say, and for the rest of the night I made myself as inconspicuous as possible while Hat and Kenneth talked. I either lapsed into unconsciousness again, or perhaps I slept, but the night passed by without further incident and inevitably dawn broke; it wasn't the end of the world or else I wouldn't be here writing about it, but as we trooped down off the hill the mood of the people was different. They were now bleary-eyed and pensive: a lot of marriages had been broken and home truths uttered; there had been one suicide and a whole heap of remorse.

I thought that that was the last of the end of the world, but Hat wouldn't have it. When we got home she said it was all in Revelations, but not having the high intellect required they'd miscalculated the dates, and it would be the following Wednesday night. I told her that no way was I going up that hill again to wait for the end, and I forbade her to go on the grounds that it was too dangerous for a woman on her own. She said she wouldn't be on her own, Kenneth was a firm believer and he would accompany her, so I couldn't really argue with that – I'd sooner him than me.

The following Wednesday they went again, and again the world continued its eternal rotation, but Hat, not being very bright, refused to accept the truth, although I'd have thought Kenneth would have more sense – after all he is a shop steward. But they went the following Wednesday and the next. Now every week he calls for her at eight o'clock, and off they go to await the end of the world. Mind, she doesn't take Scrabble – just a small suitcase with her toilet things. Meanwhile I sit at home by the telly, openly amazed at how thick some people can be.

THE FOOTBALL MATCH

Reminiscences. 'Hände hoch!' I shouted, but it wasn't Hitler after all.

I once wanted a day off work; not a massive problem you might think, because in the present industrial climate if you want a day off you just don't bother to go in, and if the manager says 'Where were you yesterday?', you simply say 'So that's your attitude is it?', and before you can say 'shop steward' he'll have his arm round your shoulders, explaining that he hadn't meant it to sound harsh, it was just that he'd missed. . . . However things were vastly different in the local newspaper office where I worked.

Hat was thrilled about me being in a newspaper office and she told everybody I was a reporter. She even bought me a green eyeshade, and Corky with his usual heavy wit referred to me as Chapman Pincher, but in actual fact I was the dogsbody; I made the tea and went out for sandwiches, and when somebody shouted 'Boy!' I ran. I didn't mind 'yes sirring' to Mr Claypole, the editor, but I drew the line at the regular reporter – a young clever dick just out of college, with enough grease on his hair to launch a medium-sized trawler. In any case I was old enough to be his father, so when he shouted 'Boy!' I used to saunter, and I never put mustard in his sandwiches, and it was only luck that he was the reporter and I wasn't.

I can remember one day smartie pants was out interviewing an old couple whose toilet had exploded – a wasted journey as it turned out because the toilet hadn't exploded, the wind had merely blown it down. Nevertheless because he was away the editor, being short-handed, sent me out to cover a wedding. I knew this was my big chance, and it wouldn't be long before I was the one shouting 'Boy!', and shiny bonce would be running, and I'd make sure he put mustard in. So with this happy prospect in mind I set off for the church with a photographer, an old dodderer whose camera looked as if it might be worth a bob or two to an antique collector, and I really got him at it. Shots of the church from all angles, views of the gravestones, and although he was moaning and groaning, I had him up in the belfry shooting down through one of the little holes that the ropes go through.

By now he was puffing and blowing so I left him up there to get his breath back while I sat in one of the back pews and watched the ceremony. I started to jot down my thoughts and I could feel the spirit moving within me, an experience that only poets will appreciate. I understood Keats and Housman, and how Longfellow must have felt when he sat under the tree and wrote 'a jug of wine and thou'. It was in this mood that I wrote my piece, and I must admit I surprised myself, for the words seemed to flow from my pencil as if guided by some superior being. I wrote of the sanctity of marriage, the tranquillity of the ancient aisles, motes of dust dancing in a shaft of sunlight, and the musty smell of old cassocks. Later, when I read it out to Hat, she was humbled; she looked at me with shining eyes and said it was the most beautiful thing she had ever heard, and she wasn't just saying that, because she made me a shepherd's pie for tea.

The editor, however, was a different kettle of fish. I stood at his desk while he raced through it. Then he went through it again more slowly. Then he sat back, looked at me and said, 'You —, you great steaming —.' We all knew he didn't mince his words, but that was a T-bone steak. One doesn't expect expressions like that from him

– after all he is a Methodist. Then he crumpled the paper up and threw it at me. 'Get out of here,' he said. 'It's useless, no good for anything unless you get caught short in the desert.'

So I was back making the tea, and jumping every time somebody shouted 'Boy!' And I must admit I'd made a fundamental mistake: I'd forgotten to get the name of the happy couple; and even worse, the photographer said I'd made him take so many useless pictures he'd run out of film before he could get a shot of them. Anyway I took the crumpled paper home with me, and Hat ironed it out. Then I sent it to the vicar, with a view to having it published in the parish magazine. So far he hasn't replied; it's no wonder the churches are empty.

Anyway this will give you some idea of the conditions under which I worked at the newspaper office – a Lipizzaner pulling a milk float. As I mentioned before, I wanted a day off to go to a football match. As you will have gathered, with an editor like mine excuses like having to go to a funeral were only valid if it happened to be your own. You may think that a football match is a piddling reason for halting the wheels of industry, but then again I'm not your ordinary fan, I am the secretary of the supporters' club at Sebastopol Rangers, and in all humility it's mainly due to my efforts that we now have nearly thirty members, so you can see that it is my duty to attend. Convinced of the reasonableness of this point of view, I tentatively broached the subject to the editor.

He looked up from his desk, and said: 'Are you asking for time off to go to the football match?'

I said: 'Of course not, me go to a football match, no sir. I was speaking hypothetically.'

He bent over his work again, and said: 'Hypothetically speaking, then, you can't go.' And that was the end of that.

The ironic thing about it was that the patent leather loaf, the young jumped-up reporter, was assigned to cover the match, and he hated football. I mean, had it been an ordinary match it wouldn't have been so bad, but this was the big one; we were drawn at home against Arsenal in the first round of the FA cup. Yes, the mighty Arsenal, can you imagine that, the Gunners playing on our ground. A day that would live in the mind for ever. The stand packed to suffocation, over four hundred people singing 'You'll never walk alone', not counting the rest of them standing round the touchline, TV cameras, a never-ending stream of cars and coaches making their way down Balaclava Road converging on the match. The traffic wasn't a problem, because luckily there is a large area of waste ground behind the stand that would serve as a car park, although opinion was divided as to whether to put the cars and coaches on the pitch and play on the car park or vice versa; I must admit the car park was flatter, but then of course the stand would be facing in the wrong direction.

However, you can see why it was imperative that I attended the match, not only because of my official capacity, but because it was a day in my life to rank with my birth, my confirmation and the pencil box I won for the egg and spoon race – not an impressive list of achievements, but mine own. The big thing now was how to get the day off, and I had to be there well before kick-off because I had to do the touchlines, and put the goal nets up. I couldn't really trust Hat with this important task; in any case she does the tea and lemons at half-time, and I must point out in all humility that we do this unpaid and don't get a penny for our efforts, though perhaps we do get a few perks – Hat brings home teabags and I usually manage to rewind a couple of toilet rolls.

Anyway everything depended on getting the day off. All the way home that night I wrestled with the problem, and as I turned into my front gate I bumped into Brigginshaw who was just coming out. Bang! I went flying right through the privet hedge.

'Oh, I didn't see you,' he said, helping me up.

I just looked at him in admiration. Well, Briggie is our left back, and I pitied the Arsenal attack that had to get round him – he was built like a brick chicken house, and besides being a footballer he's also our coalman. Anyway, before I could get my breath back he was on his cart and rumbling off down the street, one of nature's gentlemen. I let myself in, and as I was hanging my coat up I said 'Just bumped into Brigginshaw.'

Hat was pouring the tea. 'Oh yes,' she said, 'where did you meet him?'

'He was just coming out of here.'

'That's right,' she said. 'I forgot, he just popped in for a minute to ask how you were.'

A lump came to my throat. What a man . . . the biggest match of his life coming up, and he's worried about me. . . . And if it wasn't for him, I doubt that Hat would be such a football fanatic. Well, he pops into our house three or four times a week when I'm at work to explain the finer points of the game to her. He's really very patient; nothing is too much trouble for him – for instance, once I came home early, and there he was in his vest and pants, showing her how to tackle an oncoming forward. Its marvellous when you think that, with a coal round and training and everything, he can still find time to help others, and foster the game he loves.

I still had to find an excuse to get to the match, and as soon as we'd got *Coronation Street* out of the way I sat down to concentrate while Hat went into the kitchen to start supper. Immediately the doorbell rang, and sure enough it was Corky. I hadn't heard Hat put the pan on, but by some mystic intuition enjoyed only by policemen of Corky's calibre he just happened to be passing.

'Ah, that smells good,' he said.

It didn't smell at all yet, because Hat hadn't even lit the gas, but it was his stock opening line. I didn't want to be bothered with Corky tonight, so I told him we'd just eaten and Hat was washing up.

'Ah well, never mind,' he said, and took an old corned beef sandwich out of his helmet.

'Look, Corky,' I said. 'We're busy tonight. We have a lot of problems to sort out for the match on Saturday.'

He choked on the first bite. 'Problems!' he said. 'You've got problems!' And he spat out the word.

Now I don't mind corned beef, but I do like it served well.

'Listen, lad,' he said. 'Saturday is my day off, but because of this stupid match I'm on football ground duty.'

I stared at him in disbelief. 'You're going to the match.'

'I've got to,' he said. 'And it was my day off.' He was so agitated that he put his sandwich down for a minute.

'Hat,' I shouted. She came in wiping her hands.

'Oh hello, Corky', she said. 'It won't be ready for half an hour yet.'

'Never mind the hash foundry,' I said. 'He's going to the match on Saturday.'

'Oh, that's nice, I'll be there too. You'll enjoy it.'

Corky exploded. 'Enjoy it?' he said. 'I'll be on duty, madam, on my day off.'

I felt sick.

Then Hat said: 'What a pity you're not in the police, Eric. You'd be able to go to the match.' She was about to go back into the kitchen when she stopped. 'Wait a minute. Corky wants a day off; you want to go to the match – there you are, then.'

Corky and I looked at each other. 'There we are where?' I said.

'Well,' said Hat. 'You're the same height as Corky. You could go in his uniform.'

Corky stopped chewing for a minute and I noticed he was into an apple now – the sandwich had gone. I turned away to look at Hat; then the choppers started again.

'It wouldn't work out,' he mumbled through crushed

apple. 'My uniform'd be much too big in the chest, and he'd never get the belt fastened.'

I let it pass. I happened to know that most of the top half of his tunic was stuffed full of provisions, and as for his waist I'd seen more than one pair of corsets on his washing line.

'In any case,' he went on, 'your brother wouldn't know the first thing about doing the job, having to wade in among that lot of yobbos swearing and screaming and having a go at one another.'

'Ah, yes,' said Hat, 'but you'll be able to get a close look at the players.'

'I'm talking about the players,' snapped Corky. 'Bunch of overgrown, overpaid kids in short pants, kicking a ball about, and half of them can't even do that properly.'

I looked at him pityingly. How could he appreciate the finer points of the game, the midfield play, the sweeper, 4-3-4 formation, set free kicks. No – his idea of a good time was to represent the police at an eating contest.

Hat stood up 'Brigginshaw, our sweeper,' she said. never seen Brigginshaw, have you?' she said.

Corky looked at her: 'Who's Brigginshaw?'

Hat stood up 'Brigginshaw, your sweeper', she said. 'And wait till you've seen him.' The dreamy look came over her face again. 'Wait till you see the muscles on his legs.'

Corky snorted: 'If I want to see a pair of legs like tree-trunks I'll ask my Elsie to lift her skirt up.' Hat was shocked. Corky realized he'd gone too far. 'Just a joke,' he said, and to compensate he went on: 'Hey, I think I know a fellow who can get your brother a ticket for the match.'

I whipped round at him: 'I've got a ticket for the match. I'm the secretary of the supporters' club. It's my job to lay out the kit for the lads and allocate the Arsenal dressing-room. I'm an integral part of the football club, and I can't go because my stupid editor won't give me the day off.' I flopped down exhausted.

Hat dashed into the kitchen, because not only smoke but a terrible smell of burnt leftovers was coming through the hatch.

Corky read the signs in a flash, and made his way to the door. 'Must be off,' he said. 'A big manor to cover.' And as a parting shot he said: 'Sorry you can't go to the match. Keep your eyes open, though, you might see me on the telly in *Match of the Day*.'

He just managed to close the door before a book smashed into it. On top of that Hat came in from the kitchen with a blackened, smoking frying pan, and asked if I'd mind a Spam sandwich. I sank into the chair, a picture of utter dejection, and to prove the old adage that it never rains but it pours, the doorbell went again and it was Mr Brown. He was beaming all over his face; it's the look he has when he knows he's got something to say that I'm going to hate. I waited while he exchanged pleasantries with Hat, like our gate's sticking again, and what was that awful smell. Hat apologised for the gate and glared at me as if I'd stuck it on purpose; then she explained about the burnt supper, and he graciously accepted her excuses, holding a handkerchief to his nose. Then he sauntered over to me with that supercilious smile on his face.

'Going to the match on Saturday?' he said.

So that was it. He'd heard that I couldn't go and here he was to rub it in. I just looked away. He perched himself on the arm of the settee and took out his cigarette case. As he selected one and placed it carefully in his cigarette holder Hat dashed forward and struck a match. Mr Brown just raised one eyebrow at her and used his lighter.

Hat blushed and pretended she was just trying the match out. She even struck another one and said, 'It's a good box, this', but I just looked at him coolly. With that cigarette holder he always fancied himself as Noel Coward; as a matter of fact there was one period when it was all Noel this and Noel that, and how he'd seen Noel only the other day. Well, I mean, there's nothing special in that – I could have seen Noel if I'd been fool enough to spend four or five quid on a supper at the Savoy. Anyway Mr Brown hadn't finished with me yet.

'Should be a good match,' he drawled.

'Oh, come on,' I said. 'What do you know about it, you've never been to a football match in your life.'

'No,' he said, smirking. 'But I'm going to this one.' My mouth fell open.

Hat was delighted. 'Oh, that's marvellous, Mr Brown,' she gushed. 'We'll be able to stand together.' He didn't even bother to look at her.

'I hardly think so,' he said. 'I've been invited to sit with the directors.' And he chuckled: 'Well, actually with the managing director.'

Hat took a pace back, mentally cursing herself for having the temerity even to think of standing next to Mr Brown. My mouth was still open. Me the secretary of the supporters' club and couldn't go; the young cub reporter and Corky both hating football but having to go as a duty; and Mr Brown, who didn't know a half back from his elbow, would be sitting on a chair on the touchline next to Mr Abrahams. I was so shattered by it all that I didn't hear Mr Brown go. When I looked up Hat was sweeping his cigarette ash into a dustpan.

'Don't worry, Eric,' she said over her shoulder. 'We'll think of a way to get you to the match.'

I was suddenly filled with a firm resolution. Come hell or high water I was going to find an excuse to get Saturday off. 'Right,' I said. 'Let's think. There must be a way.'

'What about your supper?'

'Never mind supper at a time like this. Think, that's all. Just think.'

For what seemed ages I paced up and down as one idea after another flashed through my head. Hat just sat there staring at the wall, and it was painful to watch her struggling with her faculties, then suddenly she shot bolt upright.

'What would happen', she said, 'if you went into the editor's office in the morning and poured a bottle of ink over him?' I stared at her for a minute.

'If I did what?'

'If you poured a bottle of ink over the editor.'

'Oh, come on, Hat,' I said. 'That's stupid. I'd be out of that office before you could say "Hold the front page".'

She was triumphant. 'Exactly,' she said. 'And you'd be free to go to the football match.' And with that she fell back in the chair, exhausted.

'But then I'd be out of a job.'

'Ah yes,' she said, 'it's not foolproof. But in any case you could go down to the tribunal on Monday and claim wrongful dismissal – some of the shipbuilders got £10,000.'

'Oh for goodness sake Hat, talk sense. This is a newspaper office, not Cammell Laird. And in any case theirs was redundancy payments and if I poured a bottle of ink over the editor he'd be within his rights to fire me.'

She came back straight away. 'Not if you tripped. You can always say it was an accident.'

Then she went a bit pale and I knew that her brain was used up for the night. I was about to ask her for a cup of cocoa before she got too weak, when inspiration struck me – as with all great minds, thoughts of brilliance come when least expected – and it was Hat's last words that had triggered off the mechanism. 'Have an accident' – I said it loud, and Hat said she'd already thought of that and added that it wasn't easy having an accident.

Now that she knew I was enthusiastic she was worried; she said 'You have to be careful if you're going to have an accident.' This is the kind of remark Hat comes out with and they sound all right at the time.

'Listen, Hat,' I said. 'Sit down. No. First of all bring the cocoa in, then I'll explain what I want you to do.' She didn't move, so I plunged straight in. 'The newspaper is situated over a chip shop in Crimea Road, and Mr Claypole's office on the first floor overlooks the road, so if I had an accident right outside he'd be the first to see it.'

Hat's mouth fell open. 'Are you serious?' she said.

'It's foolproof, Hat.'

She stared at me. 'You mean you wait until Mr Claypole is looking out of the window, then you just step off the kerb under a bus?'

'Not quite,' I said. 'Not a bus – a car. And you . . .' I said, pausing for effect, '. . . will be driving it.'

'No fear,' she said. 'I'd lose my no claim bonus.'

I turned away as if disinterested. I knew the penny hadn't dropped yet, and she hadn't quite realized the enormity of what I was asking her to do. I was patient; in about two or three hours she'd suddenly stand stock still and say, 'You want me to knock you down in the car?' Well, once having got over that hurdle I could explain the rest of the plan, but by golly I underestimated her this time – in less than ten minutes after her no claim bonus bit she stood stock still and said, 'You want me to knock you down in the car?'

I nodded and she said, 'Oh, Eric.' Now Hat has different ways of saying 'Oh, Eric.' There's 'Oh, Eric!' when I come home late after having a few; there's 'Oh, Eric!' if I suggest I'm going to skate round the world in eighty days; there's 'Oh, Eric' if for instance I was accepted at the golf club; but this 'Oh, Eric' was a new one, so I pressed on in case it was counter-productive.

'Listen, Hat,' I said. 'Listen, will you.' She folded her arms and waited. I carried on. 'You'll be parked about twenty yards away, right? And I'll come out of the office. Now when I give you the signal drive up and clap the brakes on – you know what a noise they make. Well, when you've stopped, I bang the bonnet and lie down. In the meantime he's heard the squeal of brakes, heard the thump, and I might give an "Ooooh" as well, but by the time he's got to the window it'll look like the classic accident.'

She didn't seem particularly impressed. 'Then what?' she said.

'Well then, he'll come down, and you'll say you never had a chance, couldn't avoid him or something like that. Then you'll say luckily you're his sister so if he wouldn't mind helping you with him into the car you'll take him home.'

She thought about it for a minute or two, then she said: 'Supposing he's standing at the window and sees me stop, then he sees you thump the bonnet and lie down in the road?'

'No way,' I said. 'It'll be dark for a start. All he'll see is headlights – the rest will be in his mind – he'll hear a thump, a crowd'll gather, and being a newspaper man he'll be downstairs like a shot.' But she hadn't quite got the picture, so I drew a diagram on a piece of paper. 'Now,' I said. 'Here is the newspaper office, X is me coming out at exactly 5.30 and Y is you parked here.'

She put her finger on Y: 'What if it's a double yellow line?'

'Listen, Hat. If you arrive at 5.29 precisely you won't be there long enough to get a ticket. Just pull in and keep your engine running, OK? Now when you get my signal – two flicks on my cigarette lighter – drive forward.'

'Leave my engine running?' she said, and I knew her thoughts were on the cost of petrol, but I didn't want her switching off, then having to start up again – when Hat gets behind the steering wheel it's a major operation. Everything has to be just right: gear lever neutral, brakes off, doors secure, seat belts fastened etc. – they spend less time doing pre-flight checks on a Boeing 747. By the time Hat was ready to roll, Mr Claypole would be home watching the Epilogue, so it was vital she didn't switch off. Hat shook her head: 'It's too dangerous.'

I shrugged. 'Well if you won't do it I'll have to take my chance with a bus.'

'And what if you get killed?' she said.

'If I can't go to the match there's no point in me going on living.'

We were quiet for a few moments, then Hat said: 'Let's go through it again.'

We had a couple of rehearsals: Hat sitting on a chair saying 5.29, me pretending to step out and flick my lighter; Hat saying, 'Acknowledge with headlamps, 5.30 move forward, clap on brakes.' I tried not to get impatient with her while she went through all these superfluous motions because Hat is a very conscientious driver, and not only was she sitting on the chair but she was pretending to put it into gear, indicator out, then arm out. She always sticks her arm out just in case they might miss the indicator – she'd put her leg out as well if the door was open; if she's in a 30 mph limit she does 30, no more no less, and in a 40 mph limit exactly 40; and she won't drive on the motorway because she says she's not competent enough to do 70. Anyway the main thing was that she was now agreeable to the scheme and I knew she would be in the same frame of mind tomorrow. She doesn't mull over an idea when she goes to bed like I do – when she hits the sack that's it, and the next thing is: 'Where am I?'

The following afternoon everything appeared to be quite normal in the office, but I was getting jittery; every half hour or so I kept hearing a squeal of brakes outside and I knew that Hat was practising. I only hoped she wouldn't run out of petrol by 5.30. Luckily Mr Claypole never looked out of the window, but just kept muttering 'Maniacs.'

I very nearly gave the game away myself – Mr Claypole suddenly looked up and said, 'For God's sake stop flickering that damn lighter. Do you want to set the office on fire?' Immediately another wild idea sprang to mind, but

I dismissed it straight away since scheme one was already in the pipeline.

It was unfortunately Friday, and it is a fact of life that 5.30 always comes slowly on Friday. After 5.30, time shoots by until Monday morning when it slows up again. However, eventually at 5.28 I said 'Goodnight, Mr Claypole,' and with a deep breath I stepped out into the street. I glanced up at the lighted window of the *Bugle*, and I could see Mr Claypole pacing up and down with a telephone in his hand. I looked at my watch: 5.29 precisely. Two quick flicks of my lighter and an answering flash from Hat's headlights and Operation Football Match was launched.

It would have worked beautifully had it not been for one of life's imponderables – women. Hat started to drive up the road towards me. As she got closer I was anticipating the squeal of brakes so I could step out, bang the bonnet, and lie down, when for some extraordinary reason instead of stepping on the brakes she put her foot down on the accelerator, and the car shot forward, missing me by inches. I stepped into the road to call after her, when there was a squeal of brakes behind and a taxi swerved right at me. He didn't actually touch me, but in moments of crisis my brain works like an ice-cold computer, and before the taxi driver could say, 'Where to, guv?' I'd banged his bonnet and lain down: 'the classic accident'. The taxi driver was out of his cab and bending over me.

'Here,' he said. 'What's the idea of thumping my bonnet like that?'

I looked up at him, and over his shoulder I saw Mr Claypole up at the window, shielding his eyes to see what was going on. I smiled weakly at the taxi driver and said, 'It's OK. Don't worry about it.'

'What do you mean, don't worry about it?' he shouted. 'I've only had that cab three weeks, and I don't take kindly to mad jacks who belt my bonnet.'

By this time a little crowd was gathering and Hat

pushed her way through. 'It's all right,' she said 'He's my brother.'

The taxi driver looked at her. 'Is he a demonstrator?'

'Oh, no,' she said.

'Well then, what's he want to lie in the road for?'

'He hasn't been very well,' she said.

He examined his bonnet again and got back in his cab. As he started up, he leaned out and shouted, 'You want to have him seen to, missus,' and with a flourish that only cabbies possess he turned right round in his own length and disappeared.

Hat crouched down by me as I lay there, and a friendly onlooker took off his mac and rolled it into a pillow. Hat took it, said, 'Thank you very much', and knelt down on it.

I gave her such a look but she was oblivious to me lying on the wet road – she was smiling up at the guy, wondering if her ship might have come in. Then I had a sudden happy vision of me hobbling into the ground tomorrow on a stick. Perhaps they'd let me sit on the trainer's bench, and people might think I was an injured player. The thought vanished as a bus went by, splashing mud all over me. I wiped my face. Where was the editor? Why wasn't he here? Supposing he didn't come down at all, supposing there was some big news coming through that very moment? It would be just my luck for the Queen to abdicate or Prince Charles to run off with the Three Degrees. I was freezing cold now and wet, and just as I was thinking of jacking it in Mr Claypole was standing over me.

'Don't worry, Sykes,' he said. 'I saw it all. Ran you down like a dog and didn't even stop. I would have been here sooner but thought it best if I had a quick shave. I've got a photographer coming.'

I looked at him blankly while Hat introduced herself. Then she asked him to give her a hand to get me into the car but Mr Claypole wouldn't hear of it.

'No, no,' he said. 'Don't move him whatever you do,'

and I felt rather shamefaced about the deception until he said, 'Well, not until my photographer gets here.' And he explained that he'd just been writing an editorial on hit-and-run drivers – the dangers of this particular road, and the need for a lighted pedestrian crossing. By this time the on-lookers were getting bored – there was no blood, and a thin drizzle was beginning to fall – the owner of the mac that Hat was kneeling on asked if he could have it back, as he was late for choir practice and the traffic was beginning to pile up. Mr Claypole looked up at his window, and said, 'I'm sorry about this, but we must have some pictures.'

Hat had a look in her mirror and put some more lipstick on. I felt a right nit lying there while she and Mr Claypole discussed the weather. I was just about to get up when the photographer dashed out.

'Where've you been?' said Mr Claypole, but as the photographer made to answer Mr Claypole cut him short. 'Never mind, get one of me holding his hand.'

The photographer jockeyed for a good angle; he nudged me with his toe and said, 'Can you turn your head a bit towards me?' and as I did so Hat bent down to be in the shot. I could have hit her – she was smiling at the camera, flash, flash, flash. One or two people came round the back to get in the picture as well. Then we had to have one of Mr Claypole with his hand on my forehead – it was stupid really, he was hiding my eyes and it could have been any-body lying there. The photographer even took a close-up of Mr Claypole and knelt on my chest to take it.

Anyway after about twelve pictures they all adjourned to the pavement to have their names and addresses taken for the paper, and I was left stuck in the road. The editor was jubilant. 'This'll make 'em sit up and think,' he said to Hat. Then another thought struck him: 'If he dies it'll make the nationals.' He clapped his hands to his mouth when he realized what he'd said, and apologised profusely to Hat, then made it worse by assuring her that in the case of death the newspaper would naturally take care of the funeral expenses.

Then the ambulance arrived. Well, that was something else I hadn't bargained for – some public-spirited fool had phoned, and here I was being carted off to Casualty. This wasn't part of my plan, and hospitals scare the living daylights out of me. Then I perked up a bit, after all there was nothing wrong with me except that I was wet through, and when they'd examined me I'd be home by ten o'clock.

However this turned out to be another miscalculation. As I lay in Casualty the doctor came in and said: 'Where does it hurt?'

I said: 'It doesn't hurt at all,' and he shook his head sadly.

Then he prodded me, and said: 'No pains at all?'

I said 'No', and he shook his head again. He was young and I could see he was dying to have a go at me. I thought for a minute of saying something like 'Well, my ankle feels a bit stiff', but when I looked at him I bit back the words. I knew if I gave him an inch that would be it, and I'd wake up in the morning with no foot.

'Um,' he said. 'There doesn't seem to be much damage, but you can never tell with these things.' He tried to look grave, but I guessed that I was probably his first professional case. I could see from his face that shaving was still a major operation.

However after going over me again with his lights and little hammers he had me packed off to a ward so the next doctor could check me out in the morning. I didn't mind. It helped my plan even more because being in hospital was authentic – the bed was fairly comfortable, the cocoa wasn't all that bad and neither was the nurse.

As she tucked me in she said, 'Everything all right?'

I smiled a tight smile. 'Don't worry about this patient, miss,' I said. 'It'll take more than a mad taxi driver to get me down.' I was just about to tell her how much I admired the nurses and what a great job they were doing when she stuck a thermometer in my mouth and went on to check my pulse. I stared up at her and she really looked good: a wave of self-pity came over me. If only I wasn't shackled to this hospital bed, a useless hulk. I turned my face away. She whipped the thermometer out and made a note on the pad.

'Would you like me to give you something to help you sleep?' she said.

'Don't worry about me sleeping,' I said. 'I slept on the Normandy beaches.'

'Oh, I haven't had my holiday yet,' she said, and turned the light out.

At three o'clock in the morning I asked her for a pill, and before I could tell her what a great job I thought nurses were doing it was Saturday morning.

I told you about Friday going slow, but that Saturday morning in hospital was really dragging its feet. It was now ten o'clock and I hadn't seen a doctor yet – for all I knew they didn't get up before eleven – and the day nurse was no help. She had arms like Jacobean table legs, and a bigger moustache than Corky's although it wasn't as neat. I was in the end bed, and next to me was a small, wizened Irishman with no teeth, who kept glancing at me and muttering, 'Queue jumpers.' Why I was supposed to be a queue jumper was beyond me, but I didn't want an argument. I pressed the bell again, and almost immediately Nurse Horseface or whatever her name was appeared.

'Get your hand off that bell,' she said. 'You've done nothing but ding it since six o'clock this morning.'

'When's the doctor coming?' I asked.

'He'll be here in his own good time,' she snapped. 'And if you put your finger on that bell one more time I'll have it disconnected, and I'm not talking about the bell.'

Then she snatched the pillow from behind me, gave it a karate chop that would have felled a fully grown ox, and stuffed it back behind my head. (The pillow, not the fully grown ox.)

'Why is he next to the window?' This from the Irishman in the next bed.

Horseface whirled round. 'Because he was put there, that's why. Now don't you start, Mr Flaherty – you're like a couple of six-year-olds.'

I tried another tack: I smiled that winning smile of mine that usually gets me a few free doughnuts at Madge's bread shop. 'Look, nurse,' I said. 'I know you're busy. Why don't I just get up and go?'

She didn't answer. She was tucking in the sheets round Mr Flaherty at the time; I hoped she wouldn't tuck mine in like that because it would have stopped my circulation.

I tried again. 'Nurse,' I said, but she cut me short.

'Sister, if you don't mind. And the reason you have to wait for the doctor is because you might be suffering from concussion.'

'Honestly, Sister, I'm not suffering from concussion.'

She stood over me: 'You touch that bell again, and you will be.'

Mr Flaherty tugged at her skirt: 'Is he a private patient?' he whined.

'No, I'm not a private patient.'

'I should be in that bed, then.'

Sister Horseface put her fists on her hips, or just about where they should have been. 'Now pack it in you. We're busy enough as it is today, we've got to get the Casualty ward ready.'

'I was in Casualty yesterday,' I said.

'You were lucky,' she snapped. 'You won't get in it today, what with the football match on. At six o'clock tonight that ward'll look like the bridge at Arnhem.' And with that she weighed anchor and set sail round the corner.

Mr Flaherty leaned over: 'And she's the nice one,' he said. 'Wait till you see the doctors.'

I picked up the newspaper and tried to read, but he wouldn't let go.

'If it's Dr Barnaby, I should watch him. He likes the knife, he does. . . . You're the concussion, aren't you?'

I ignored him.

'Oh, yes,' he went on. 'I should watch him. He won't just shine a light in your eyes and move his fingers, he'll have your head open.'

I put my paper down. 'Do you mind?' I said. 'I'm trying to read.' I might just as well have saved my breath.

He looked round, then leaned towards me conspiratorially. 'If they come to shave your head, don't let 'em,' he said. 'They have to shave your head first, then they paint it purple. One slash of the knife and they're in.' He shook his head sadly. 'It's like a playground to them. Fiddle about they do, then they stitch you up, and sometimes they don't put it all back.' He folded his arms and looked at me knowingly.

'They didn't put *any* of yours back.' I didn't say it too loud because although he couldn't have been more than eight stone and was ill, the Irish can be very touchy, and I didn't fancy a brawl in my hospital nightie. I mean you're covered down the front – but they economize on the back. He was shaking his head again.

'If they ask you to sign a paper, don't, because you have to sign a paper saying it's all right, and once you've signed that they're laughing.'

I turned on my side away from him and tried to concentrate on the sports page. It was quiet for a moment, and I was tempted to look over my shoulder to see if he'd gone to sleep. No such luck.

'Anything happening outside at all?' he said.

It was then I realized that a little above me was a window, and if I knelt on the bed I could just see down the street.

'What's the traffic like?' he said.

'Oh, it's piling up.' The scene was a typical few hours-before-the-match one. Mobs of red and white scarves were careering about arm in arm, waving bottles; shopkeepers were boarding up their windows and just up the street one or two of the lads were leaping from roof to roof on the parked cars. Right opposite another knot of supporters were playfully trying to overturn a coachload of rival supporters. I lay back in bed.

'What's happening?' he said.

'Not a lot.' I went back to my paper.

'Is there a bus outside?' he said.

I got up to the window and looked up and down. 'Yes, there's a bus,' I said, and lay back again.

'Oh, yes,' he said. 'That'll be the twenty past. I was on that route for six years before they put the Pakis on.'

I didn't quite understand what he meant by 'putting the Pakis on', but I certainly wasn't going to encourage him. I read a little more about the side that Arsenal would be fielding that day, and I'd just got to Liam Brady's hamstring injury when he piped up again.

'Which way was it going?'

I lowered the paper. 'Which way was *what* going?' I asked.

'The bus,' he said. 'The bus outside.'

'It wasn't going anywhere,' I said. 'It was stopped.'

He sucked his cheeks in till his mouth was the size of a collar stud while he studied his watch, then he said: 'Which way was it facing?'

I got up to the window again. 'It's still stopped,' I said over my shoulder.

'Would it be facing that way at all?' he said, and pointed.

'Yes,' I told him, and fell back on my pillows.

'It won't be the twenty past, then,' he said. 'Where the devil is he off to?'

I tried to get back to Liam Brady's hamstring.

'Unless its Earls Court to Kilburn, but then he'd be miles off his route. It's not a blackie driving, is it?'

I dashed the paper down. 'We're four floors up,' I said. 'I haven't got bionic eyes.'

'I've got good eyes,' he said. 'I've always had good eyes. Oh yes, sir, and I wouldn't have to look in the cab to know if it was a blackie – I can tell by the way he drives.'

'Well that one's still standing there,' I said, and flung myself back on the bed. He cocked his head on one side, then he cupped one hand to his ear.

'That's a bus,' he said. 'Is it a bus going past?'

'Oh, for goodness sake,' I said. 'Get in here,' and I hopped out of bed and helped him into mine.

'Oh, thanks,' he said. 'You're a gentleman. Only I should have had this bed anyway, I was here first.'

I climbed into his bed and settled back.

'There's the twenty past now,' he said. 'Five minutes late; I'll bet it's a Paki on that.'

I put my paper down. 'Look, Mr er – '

'Flaherty,' he said, 'Seamus Flaherty.'

'Well then, Mr Flaherty, you've got the bed you wanted, so just leave me in peace to read my paper while you look out of the window.'

'It's not allowed,' he said. 'If the sister catches you at it there's hell to pay,' and with that he settled down and before I could lift my paper again his eyes closed and he was fast asleep.

My finger went to the bell again to ask about the doctor, but I changed my mind. I still had a couple of hours in hand before I made my way to the ground. I lay on my side and thought about the afternoon. I saw me on the touchline watching the players run out for a pre-match kick-around, and a sudden panic gripped me – I hoped Arsenal had brought plenty of balls with them, because we only had about three and they'd need a good wash down before we could use them. I saw myself being introduced to the manager of Arsenal: 'This is Mr Sykes, one of our stalwarts of the club.' I must have been dozing, because just before the match the referee was taken ill and they asked me to take over. I was just spinning the coin when one of the players pinched me playfully on the backside; it wasn't pleasant – it was a sharp pain – and I jerked upright.

'Steady on, you'll wreck the needle.' I looked round, and there was a young nurse I hadn't seen before putting a hypodermic syringe in the pan.

'What are you doing?' I said, pulling the bedclothes up.

'It's all over now,' she said. 'We'll come for you in a few minutes.'

'What's all over? I'm waiting to see the doctor,' I said.

'And he's waiting to see you, so just lie back and relax.'

I lay back and looked at her, but she didn't seem to be quite in focus. A warm feeling was creeping over me, and I tried to tell her what a grand job I thought the nurses were doing but I didn't seem to be able to frame my words. I didn't really care, though; I heaved a deep sigh of content and the next thing I vaguely remember was two fellows in white lifting me on to a trolley, corridor lights flashing by, and then it was goodnight Vienna.

About half an hour later Nurse Horseface strode into the ward and began to strip down the bed I'd been in. Suddenly she whipped round and stared down at the white, pinched face of Old Ireland with its moaning little black hole of a mouth; she shook it roughly. He struggled to open his eyes and saw Horseface bending over him: 'Glory be,' he said, 'it's the devil himself.'

'Never mind that, Mr Flaherty,' she said. 'What are you doing in this bed?'

'Nothing,' he replied. 'It's as clean as the day I got in.'

'What I mean is,' she said, 'where's the suspected concussion, who should be here?'

'Ah, him,' said Flaherty. 'Ah well, you see he forced me to get into his bed so he could pop into mine. Said he couldn't stand the noise of the traffic.'

She looked round at the empty bed and steadied herself on the side table. 'Good grief,' she moaned. 'They've taken him up. There'll be hell to pay for this,' and she lolloped down the ward.

Meanwhile at home Hat was beginning to get a little agitated. You'd think that instead of sitting there taking the stuffing out of a cushion she'd have phoned the hospital to find out what was going on, but that's Hat – she doesn't want to bother anybody. However even Hat has a breaking point, and she was just about to look up the hospital number when the doorbell went. Her face lit up, then fell again; it was Constable Turnbull.

'Oh, Corky,' she said. 'Eric isn't back yet. Only an hour to kick-off and he'll have to change and everything. I've laid out his Union Jack suit and his Thermos is ready and I've – ' she stopped in mid-sentence, for Corky was smiling in a peculiar way. 'Wait a minute,' she said. 'Shouldn't you be on duty at the match?'

He carefully selected an orange from the fruit bowl. 'I've got out of that,' he said, 'thanks to you and your brother.'

'Oh, that's nice,' she said. 'Oh, that's good, because I have to go and sort out the tea and lemons and stuff for half-time, so here's Eric's ticket. When he comes tell him I've gone on, and – ' Corky held up his hand and Hat stopped.

'I'm sorry,' he said, popping the last of the orange into his mouth. 'But you won't be going to the match.'

Hat's jaw dropped. 'Why not?'

He licked his fingers and started to peel a banana. 'I'm afraid, madam, I must ask you to accompany me to the station.'

Hat gripped him by the wrist so hard the banana went splat on the ceiling, leaving him holding the soggy skin. 'It's not Eric, is it? Has anything happened? It's not to identify him, is it?'

'Just keep calm, madam. It's not your brother, it's you.'

'Me?' she said. 'And don't wipe your hand on the settee, use your hankie. What have I done?'

He looked at her steadily. 'It's customary, madam,' he said, 'after an accident to report it to the police.'

'I didn't have an accident. That was Eric.'

'I know who it was, and what happened, because I watched it all from a shop doorway.' Hat stepped back.

'You watched it all! You saw an accident in the street and you didn't come forward to help, you, a policeman?'

Corky was thrown off balance for a minute. 'I had my hands full,' he said.

'Yes – fish and chips.'

'Did you see me?' he blurted, then realized his mistake. 'Look, Hattie,' he said pleadingly. 'You don't understand. It's not just rendering first aid and keeping the crowd back when there's an accident. We have to take notes, then there's forms to fill in and then we have to go to court, and it's always on a day off. So once you start rushing out for every Tom Dick or Harry that gets knocked down there's no end of it.'

She moved away from him. He didn't like her expression.

'Look, Hattie, all you have to do is come down to the station with me. We'll clear it all up in no time, and I won't have to go to the match.'

Hat pinned on her rosette and picked up her rattle. 'But I want to go to the match, and that's where I'm going when Eric gets here.'

Corky was exasperated. 'But he's in hospital, Hattie. Good grief, I heard the bang when he got knocked down. I'm surprised he wasn't killed outright – any normal man would have been.' He stopped suddenly and turned sharply towards her. 'Haven't you phoned the hospital to see how he is?'

Hat was flustered. 'Well, no. Well, I mean, he seemed all

right last night. Well, he was quite lucid,' she faltered. 'I'd better ring now, hadn't I?' and she started to dial.

Corky was dumbfounded. 'By jingo, you can be hard when you want to be.'

Hat reddened. 'Hello,' she said. 'Yes, please. Can I speak to someone about Mr Sykes -- Sykes. No, Sykes with a Y.'

Corky pretended not to be listening, but no one examines an apple that closely.

Hat went on: 'No, I don't know what ward he's in. He was admitted last night. They took him in an ambulance. That's right: "Sykes".' She listened for a moment, then gripped the phone with both hands. 'They've what!' she said. Then she staggered slightly and her face went the colour of three-day-old snow. She put the phone down and stared at Corky.

'Well?' he said.

'They've taken his tonsils out.'

'His tonsils.' Corky was dumbfounded. 'He wasn't hit in the face, was he?'

Hat recovered slightly. After all, I'd spent my whole life being unpredictable so the shock was only temporary. She decided to make a clean breast of it. 'There wasn't an accident, Corky,' she said. 'It was just an excuse, so that Eric could have the afternoon off to see the match.'

Corky couldn't believe his ears. 'Are you telling me he hired a taxi to knock him down, so he could have the day off?'

'Well, no,' she said. 'The taxi *was* an accident. What I mean is, I was supposed to knock him down, but I missed. The taxi was a bit of luck. No, I mean we didn't plan the taxi, but if he hadn't come when he did Eric wouldn't have been knocked down. Well, he wasn't knocked down actually. Well, what I mean is – ' Hat was desperately floundering now, but before she could really confuse him the doorbell rang. It was Mr Claypole, the editor.

'Ah,' he said, coming straight to the point. 'Can I see your brother?'

'I'm afraid not,' she said. 'He's still in hospital.'

Mr Claypole looked at his watch. 'He can't still be in there. He wasn't badly hurt, was he? He walked to the ambulance all right, and I've seen some of the photos we took – he was smiling, with his thumb up.'

Hat nodded. 'He wasn't badly hurt, but they've taken his tonsils out.'

Mr Claypole looked at Corky, then back at Hat. 'That's typical, that is,' he exploded. 'Ever since he's been with the paper I've looked after him, treated him kindly, turned a blind eye when he comes in late, and this is how he repays me – he goes and has his tonsils out the one day when I need him.'

'Well, I'm sorry,' said Hat, 'but if there's anything I can do. . . .'

Mr Claypole snorted. 'You,' he said. 'Your brother's no gift to the newspaper, but at least he knows what I want. But that's typical – he's let me down again.'

'What do you want him to do?' said Hat.

'My reporter,' breathed Mr Claypole, 'another useless appendage, fell down the stairs as he was leaving the office and is still unconscious. He happened to be on his way to report on the football match. This left me with no option but to send your brother in his place. However your brother calmly decides to have his tonsils out.'

Hat sat down suddenly. 'And that's why you're here?' she said in a small voice.

He glared at her for a moment. 'Eh?' he said.

She looked at him in amazement. 'You want Eric to report on the match.'

He slammed his hat on. 'That was the general idea. Now I've got to go myself, and believe me there's a million things I'd rather be doing than spending an afternoon at a football match.' And with that he stormed off to the ground.

Corky started to chuckle and Hat rounded on him. 'I don't see what there is to laugh about,' she said.

Corky tried not to laugh outright. 'That's your brother all over, one scheme after another. If he'd have let things take their natural course he'd have been at the match now, and with a full set of tonsils.' With that he sat back and laughed and laughed till his dentures fell out.

'Those are British legs, Hat.'

MR BROWN

I can never imagine Mr Brown, our next door neighbour, ever being young. We've known him twenty years, and although I've acquired a few more lines around the eyes, and Hat's expanded a bit, he's exactly the same. I think he must have been born with a bowler hat and glasses on, and he suits a bowler hat because he doesn't really have a head. When he takes his hat off that's it, his face finishes and there's nothing – you keep thinking the top of his head's still in his hat. To give him his due I've never seen him untidy – black jacket and striped trousers during the week, and tweeds and cravat at the weekend. Always impeccable, never a hair out of place, and if I had five minutes to spare I could count them.

What he does for a living is beyond me. Hat think's he a civil servant, but, as I pointed out, a dustman is a civil servant. Hat retorted: 'In which case he wouldn't go to work every day in a bowler hat and striped trousers', but that's where I think she's wrong. If Mr Brown was a coal miner he'd go to work in a bowler hat and striped trousers. He'd be as out of place in a pair of overalls as Hat would in a dinner jacket.

She has romantic notions about him – not earthy, or in any way to do with sex, and here I feel I'm partly to blame. I should have talked to her years ago about sex, but it's too late now, and it hasn't affected her really; she's still cheerful, and cooks well, which goes to prove that carnal knowledge isn't as important as the telly makes out. In any case she prefers reading to watching the telly, and her favourite books are all about knights and maidens, forests, madrigals and stuff like that, but for knights and barons she visualizes Mr Brown; she hasn't said as much, but I know my sister. She reads a few chapters, then leans back and closes her eyes, and I've only got to look at her to know what's going on in her head. The sun is sparkling through the greenwood, the birds are singing, and up to our rude dwelling rides Mr Brown, spurs jingling, plumes dancing on his purple hat, and eyes smiling benevolently behind his glasses. Hat greets him with a curtsey, and offers him a Banbury cake and Malmesbury ale from a cool stone flagon. After refreshment he feels in his gauntlet and throws her down a groat. She catches it and blushes with pleasure. Then I'd have to touch my forelock, take hold of his stirrup, and run alongside all the way to Windsor, so I could hold his horse while he dismounted. I know she indulges in these fantasies because once the coalman's horse trotted by outside; straightaway she got up and started to straighten her hair, then she saw me looking at her and blushed like mad. Anyway that's how she sees Mr Brown, and its understandable – he does treat her like an unpaid servant, and he looks upon me as one of the reasons we lost the Empire. The thing is he's always popping into our house, like the Duke of Edinburgh visiting a depressed area; but on the other hand we've only ever been to his house once.

We hadn't seen him for about a week, and Hat was wondering whether he was all right, so I said: 'Go and have a look', but Hat wanted me to come as well – she didn't think it right and proper to visit him alone. I agreed, too readily as it turned out because I not only had to accompany her, but I had to shave and put on my best suit. In the meantime Hat made a lovely meat and potato pie, then we popped round and knocked on his door. He opened it, but insteand of standing aside and saying, 'Come in', he just said 'Yes?' Well, Hat looked at me and I looked at my feet; I felt like a carol singer in October. The upshot of it was that we never got indoors, but the meat and potato pie did, and to this day we've never even got the dish back.

The more he treats Hat like a scullery maid the more she seems to like it. He continually asserts his superiority. For instance once Hat bought a vase, and when she showed it to him he gave it a cursory glance, one eyebrow went up, and he said: 'It's very nice, even if it is cheap, and it'll suit your house.'

Hat flushed. 'Do you really like it, Mr Brown?'

'I wouldn't have it in my house,' he said. 'I'm afraid when one's been used to Ming it rather spoils you for bric à brac.'

'You've never had a Ming,' I said.

He looked at me as if I was sucking my thumb. 'One doesn't have to own a Rembrandt to appreciate art.'

Well, that's the sort of thing he comes out with; it's really what he *doesn't* say that counts. I swear that Hat thinks his house is stuffed with priceless art treasures and Chippendale and stuff, but he doesn't cut any ice with me; I can always get him going. I remember once, Hat was thinking of buying about five pounds' worth of shares in a new carpet cleaning company, and Mr Brown was saying as how it was a bull market and depressed at the moment, and blue chips were firm.

Hat was hanging on to his every word, while I pretended to read my newspaper. Suddenly I said: 'I see the Council are going to build a supermarket at the back of Wimbourne's in the High Street.'

Straightaway he came back with: 'Ah yes, but it's only in the pipeline. Once it gets to the committee stage I'll have something to say about it.' He turned and looked out of the window.

Hat looked at me as if to say, 'There!'

I put my paper down. 'What can you do about it?'

He turned round. 'I'm not without influence, you know.'

I paid out a little more rope. 'I'm talking about that piece of land behind Wimbourne's.'

He smiled knowingly, and accepted another cup of tea. 'I know what you're talking about,' he said patiently. 'But it has to go through the committee.' He stirred his tea. 'Before it reaches that stage I may make a phone call to a certain person. I have my own ideas on how to develop that plot.'

Hat looked at him like he was the first light on the Christmas tree.

He gulped down his cup and said: 'Well, I must be off.'

Hat rushed to open the door for him. She always did this, and he took it as his due. I believe that if she didn't open the door for him one day he'd walk right into it.

As he was about to leave, he turned and said: 'Don't bank on them building a supermarket on that piece of land.' Then he went.

Hat closed the door, then picked up Mr Brown's cup and saucer reverently. I wondered whether she'd wash them or have them framed.

'He's pathetic,' I said.

Hat put the things down again. 'You always have to denigrate him, don't you?'

I didn't reply. 'Denigrate' had floored me for the moment.

Hat went on: 'Mr Brown has more influence in his little finger than you have in your whole body.'

'Oh, come on, Hat,' I said. 'He's a bluffer. He's got as much influence as King Canute had when he sat on the beach at Blackpool.'

She looked at me pityingly. 'That's all you know,' she said. 'Well, I'll tell you this, Eric. If Mr Brown says they won't build a supermarket on that piece of land at the back of Winbourne's you can bet your life they won't build one.' Then she swept into the kitchen.

I sat there and waited, and sure enough some time later she came back slowly. I pretended to be having five minutes, but I watched her under half-closed lids.

'That waste ground at the back of Wimbourne's?' she said.

'What?' I opened my eyes.

'There isn't any waste ground at the back of Wimbourne's. They built a hotel on it last year.'

'I know,' I said, and I smiled.

Well, you would have thought Hat would have laughed too, but she didn't. She gave me such a rucking for being deceitful, and stringing Mr Brown along. I just use him for mental exercise.

Anyway that's the kind of man he is, and I appreciate that he probably went to a better school than I did, and he had a nanny and a hoop and all that jazz, but I have a natural intelligence, and I know without a doubt that, had I been blessed with Mr Brown's advantages, I wouldn't be living in Sebastopol Terrace. The world would have been my oyster, and I'm not ruling out the possibilities of the premiership. Anyway, the one-upmanship battle between us became as natural in our lives as eating and sleeping; I won a few, and he won a few – not many, but enough to keep the war going.

However one day a real bit of luck fell on me – the labour exchange offered me a job as a drinks waiter at the Parthenon. Now the Parthenon is just about the most exclusive club in London, patronized by politicians, film stars and ambassadors, but mainly its membership consisted of explorers, generals, tea planters and so on; in fact it had been founded for people of high rank who had spent most of their lives abroad, in the service of King and Country or Empire. Naturally even to be a temporary waiter I had to have impeccable references, but then I've got a drawer full of them at home, written painstakingly by my own hand and covering just about every contingency apart from the obvious ones like captaining a jumbo jet or being a bishop. The signatures on my references were all those of impressive personages of the highest rank, and all recently dead.

So I found myself serving drinks to the mighty in the hallowed precincts of the Parthenon. Naturally I didn't tell Hat I was a temporary drinks waiter. I just dressed smartly every evening and said I was off to my club. And she really is very thoughtful – as I was away every evening I slept most of the day, and do you know what that sister of mine did? She refused to have the plumber in, the coal-man, the electrician – in fact no one was allowed to work in the house during the day, and they all had to come in the evening when I was out. Hat arranged this so I wouldn't have my rest disturbed and there can't be many people like that. Also such is the respect which these fellows have for my sister that not one of them puts in a bill. It really makes me humble.

Anyway, it wasn't long before Mr Brown got wind of me and the club. It was about six in the evening, and I was just on the verge of leaving, when Hat opened the door and let him in. He stopped short when he saw me in the smart suit and the tie, which could have meant something but in fact was part Eton, part Royal Artillery and part egg.

'Off to your club, Sykes?' was Mr Brown's opening gambit.

'Of course,' I replied, brushing a crumb off my lapel. 'Enoch's coming tonight, so it should be amusing.'

Mr Brown glanced suspiciously at Hat, who just smiled proudly back at him.

'Enoch Powell?' he said.

'Who else?' I replied, looking at myself in the mirror. 'Always good for a laugh is Enoch – but intelligent, my God what a brain. As a matter of fact Duggie rates him our greatest intellectual.'

'Duggie?' asked Mr Brown.

'Douglas Bader. Now there's a fellow for you, still plays a fair game of golf and has his caddie panting to keep up with him.'

Mr Brown assumed his crafty look. 'Funnily enough,' he said, 'I'm going past the Parthenon. Perhaps I can give you a lift?'

'No, that's all right, Mr Brown. I don't mind the bus – we're all equal now, you know.'

His eyes gleamed. He thought he had me. 'I insist,' he said. 'After all, I have a car, and what are neighbours for?'

I pretended to ponder for a moment, then I said: 'Well, if it's not too much trouble,' and with that we left.

As we walked to the front gate a man came in with a bottle under his arm and passed us. Hat was still standing at the front door. 'Oh hello, Mr Ballywell,' she said. 'That washing machine of ours is still playing up.' Then they went indoors.

All the way to the Parthenon Mr Brown was pumping me, but I was self-deprecating. 'Oh, it's only a club. There are thousands of 'em in London. This one just happens to suit me.' Eventually we pulled up at the Parthenon, but I just sat there.

Mr Brown gave me a sly look. 'Aren't you going to go in, Sykes?' he said, silkily.

I played him on beautifully. 'Oh, I don't know. It's a lovely night – I may have a stroll first.'

He whirled on me in triumph. 'You daren't go in, dare you? I thought so', he sneered. 'I knew all along it was a pack of lies.'

'What was?' I asked, all innocence.

'You and the Parthenon.'

I just smiled sadly at him. Then the doorman, resplendent in his uniform, came down the steps and opened the car door. 'Good evening, Jack,' I said, and he saluted. He was an ex-sergeant-major and saluted everything, but being deaf as a post never spoke. I stepped out of the car and said: 'Has Mr Powell arrived yet?' He stared a foot above my head and saluted. 'Thank you, Jack,' I said. Then I popped my head into the car and thanked Mr Brown for the lift. I wish I could have got a picture of his expression as I disappeared into the august entrance of the Parthenon. Incidentally I got a rocket for not using the back entrance, but it had been more than worth it.

The next few weeks were among the most enjoyable in my life. It seemed that Mr Brown was never out of our house, but the positions were reversed – I sat there aloof, while he jumped up and offered cigarettes, and he even brought a bottle of port round one Sunday. He didn't call me Sykes – nor did he call me Eric come to that – but he couldn't bring himself to address me as Mister because his superiority was too ingrained. We were even invited to dinner one night at his house, so he could introduce me to the captain of the golf club. I declined politely, saying I had arranged to have dinner at the Parthenon.

'But this could mean automatic selection to the golf club – you'd be a member like that.' He tried to snap his fingers. 'You'd go through on the nod.'

I picked up the *Financial Times*, which was a recent innovation in our household but an invaluable one. 'My dear Mr Brown,' I sighed, 'when I want to join a golf club it'll be the Royal and Ancient', and I terminated the conversation by disappearing behind the paper.

He moved to a chair where he could see my face, then he fidgeted a little, offered me a cigarette, which I declined, and waited. 'Look here,' he wheedled, 'we're neighbours and I hope we're friends.' He looked at Hat for support.

'We are friends, Mr Brown. We've always admired you, haven't we, Eric?'

I continued to read, then I looked up. 'What's that?' I enquired.

'We're friends,' said Hat.

'Oh yes,' I replied, then returned to the business section.

'The point is,' blurted Mr Brown, 'well, I was wondering – could I be your guest at the Parthenon?' He looked eagerly at Hat. 'I'll pay of course, it's just that, well, I have several influential friends as you know, but I've never actually had the pleasure of meeting Enoch Powell and Lord Carrington and such like.'

I put the paper down slowly. I was really enjoying the moment; it was marvellous to see him grovelling at my feet – if I'd said 'Show me your legs?' he'd have been up on the table like a shot with his trousers over his arm.

'The point is, Mr Brown, we have to be very careful who we bring into the Parthenon, as you will appreciate. Secondly, politicians don't often come into the club – they have their own club at Westminster. Our main clientele consists of old army colonels, old India wallahs, explorers. It can be very dull sometimes when they get yarning about Cawnpore, the White Highlands or the staff problems in Nanking. When they start chewing the colonial fat I usually sit in the corner with a good book and an old brandy. I'd take you like a shot, but I mean what references do you have? I mean, what clubs do you belong to?'

'I'm a member of the golf club,' he said defiantly.

I smiled. 'It's hardly pukka, is it? We're talking about the Parthenon, not a wooden hut full of steaming socks and old golf sweaters.'

He just smiled sheepishly and offered me another cigarette.

However after a few weeks of this I was getting fed up. It's nice to be in the driving seat, but this was no contest, and I longed for the old days of his shaky superiority being brought down time after time by my acid wit. It's nice to have a dog who sits and walks to heel, and never messes the house, but I prefer one to show its teeth now and again, to get the adrenalin going, sharpening up the old reflexes.

It all came to a head one evening at the Parthenon. I'd just come out of the kitchen after a crafty swig at the vintage port. As I glanced round the room to see if anybody required service my gaze homed in on a bald head showing above the back of one of the leather armchairs. I knew the back of that head and it didn't belong to a member. It was Mr Brown's – but surely it couldn't be. There were two other fellows sitting with him and one of them beckoned me over. I stood stock still for a moment, wondering what to do. Should I slip out the back way and never come back? Whatever I did my cover was blown; and anyway what difference did it make – I'd just be back holding on to his stirrup while he rode to Windsor.

The man beckoned again impatiently, and as I squared my shoulders and came forward I decided on a cool approach. Mr Brown didn't notice me at first; he had that intelligent listening look on his face that he adopts when he's out of his depth. The man ordered three large whiskies, and I said 'Yes, sir.' Mr Brown looked at me sharply, and as enlightenment dawned he chuckled softly. I took the order to the barman, then slipped into the hall and looked at the visitors' book. There he was, a guest of Mr Lindstrom. He'd obviously crawled all over London looking for a member to take him in, and probably caught Mr Lindstrom in an unguarded moment. My heart sank to my boots. Mr Brown would get even now for all the weeks he'd been forced to eat humble pie. Hat and I would have this little incident stuffed up our noses for months to come. In fact I may never be able to regain the ascendancy. As I served their drinks the joy was oozing out of Mr Brown, and there was a newborn confidence in his attitude.

I hovered about, emptying ashtrays and flicking tables, in order to pick up snippets of conversation. I'll give him his due, he really knows how to join in; he doesn't tell lies, but he leads people to think he knows what he's talking about, for instance . . .

'Do you remember that summer in Peshawar in '47?' said Mr Lindstrom.

Mr Philimore the other man in the group, replied: 'Will I ever forget it.'

They both looked at Mr Brown, who swilled the ice round his glass, and nodded sagely. 'I'll tell you one thing,' he said. 'I doubt if it will ever be as hot again.'

Mr Lindstrom looked up sharply. 'No, no, old boy, 1947 – freak summer, lot of cloud, rain, blasted cold, you know.'

Mr Brown looked round to see if I might have overheard his gaffe, then he smiled at his host: 'Oh, *forty*-seven.'

'Shocking weather,' nodded Mr Philimore. 'We all trooped off to Simla to get warm.'

'Ah, Simla,' chimed in Mr Brown. 'There's the place if you like hot weather.'

'Who likes hot weather?' snorted Lindstrom. 'Simla's the only blasted place within striking distance one can escape the hot weather.' He eyed Mr Brown over the rim of his glass. 'Do you like Simla?'

Mr Brown didn't bat an eyelid: 'Well, I don't quite know if I like it,' he said quite truthfully.

'Good for the memsahib,' said Philimore.

'I never married,' said Mr Brown, 'so that problem didn't arise.' And he winked at Lindstrom and sipped his drink.

You have to admire him sometimes. After all he's not telling lies but he gives the impression he's a master of his subject. Here he was, an expert on India already, and I happen to know that his only overseas duty was on a bottle of cognac at Boulogne.

He snapped his fingers and said 'Boy', then he apologized. 'So sorry,' he said to his companions. 'Difficult to break the habit of a lifetime. Same again,' he said, 'and make them large ones.' I looked at the other two for confirmation and they nodded. I was secretly delighted that Mr Brown had made a gaffe. After all he was a guest, and only members could sign for drinks. Mr Lindstrom looked at Philimore and they both looked at Mr Brown, but he was quite oblivious and floating about on his cloud nine. As I was at the bar getting the drinks I missed a chunk of the conversation, but I heard Mr Brown laughing and saying: 'He'd never gone in for pig sticking.' Well, he's truthful again – there's not a lot of opportunity for pig sticking in our street.

However when I got back with the whisky the atmosphere had changed; there was a nip in the air and Mr Philimore leaped to his feet. 'Good Lord, is that the time?' he said as he gulped down his drink signed the chit and shook hands with Mr Lindstrom. 'Must dash, Bunny old boy', he said. 'Don't forget Friday.' Then he nodded to Mr Brown and left. Mr Brown sat down unabashed by his curt dismissal; I don't think it even registered.

'His face is very familiar,' said Mr Brown, 'but I can't recall having met him in India.'

Lindstrom sipped his drink. 'Hardly surprising,' he said. 'India's a big place – a damn big place. In any case Philimore spent most of his life in Singapore.'

Mr Brown leaned back luxuriously and crossed his legs. 'Ah, Singapore,' he sighed.

'Know it?' said Lindstrom.

'Who doesn't?' countered Mr Brown. He leaned forward. 'And some know it better than others,' he smirked, as if he knew every back street and every Chinese restaurant on the coast. 'There's some magic about Singapore. I've often thought I might settle down there.'

Lindstrom snorted. 'It smells,' he said.

'Ah, yes', said Mr Brown. 'I wouldn't buy a place in a smelly part. I was thinking of more up-country.'

'Rangoon?'

'Oh, no', said Mr Brown. 'Not as far up as that. Rangoon can be pretty smelly in the summer, take it from me.' He'd a few large drinks by this time and he hadn't noticed that

Mr Lindstrom was looking at him rather quizzically. 'Were you long in Singapore?' said Mr Brown. 'I mean, did you spend much time there?'

'A year,' said Mr Lindstrom.

'Just a visitor really,' chortled Mr Brown.

Mr Lindstrom looked at his watch: '. . . And you?'

'Me what?' said Mr Brown.

'Army?'

'Yes', said Mr Brown – again the truth, but I happened to know he'd been a corporal in the RAMC, and did only six months at Catterick before he was invalided out with fallen arches.

Mr Lindstrom looked hard at Mr Brown and said: 'When you were in Singapore what did you make of the Raffles?'

'The raffles?' said Mr Brown blankly.

'The Raffles in Singapore.'

'Ah, yes,' said Mr Brown. 'They don't interest me at all. I'm not really a gambling man.'

Mr Lindstrom stared at him, and Mr Brown felt obliged to carry on: 'Normally I have a pound on the Christmas raffle in the office, but that's all.'

Mr Lindstrom stood up. 'Will you excuse me a moment?'

'Certainly, old boy,' said Mr Brown, and waved his arm, which was unfortunate as his cigarette flew out of its holder and struck Mr Lindstrom.

'I'm sorry,' said Mr Brown, but by this time he was addressing Mr Lindstrom's back as he disappeared.

Mr Brown looked quickly at me, and I wiped the smile off my face. He looked round and saw we were alone. 'So this is your club, Sykes,' he said, and he smirked. 'I knew all the time you only worked here. Mr Lindstrom is putting me up for membership.' I started to polish one of the glasses.

'How did you get to know Mr Lindstrom?' I said.

'Don't be impertinent,' he snapped. 'I know a lot of people. I told you I wasn't without influence.' He sat back and sighed; he was in heaven. He was just deciding whether he should have another drink when a shadow fell across him.

'Excuse me, are you accompanied?'

Mr Brown looked up. 'Are you addressing me?' he said.

'I'm the secretary, sir.'

'Ah, of course. I'm with Mr Lindstrom.'

'I'm sorry, Mr Lindstrom left the club two minutes ago.'

Mr Brown's mouth fell open. 'But we're going into dinner in a moment.'

'I'm sorry, sir, but Mr Lindstrom said he wouldn't be back.'

Mr Brown floundered. 'But he can't. I mean – '

The secretary was polite but firm. 'I'm sorry, sir, but the rules plainly state that you cannot remain on the premises unless accompanied by a member, so I'm afraid I must ask you to leave.'

Mr Brown's face went brick red, and he rose and left the room without looking back. For the first time in my life I really felt sorry for him. Three weeks later I got the elbow – stupid really, with all the money in that club they actually count the bottles of port. However Mr Brown and I have a tacit agreement: the name of the Parthenon is never mentioned.

THE LAST BUS HOME

Our first house — they said passing trains would make no difference.

A funny thing happened on the last bus home one Saturday night a good many years ago. If you read it in a book you wouldn't believe it, but it's true. It had been the usual dreary Saturday night dance at the local Palais. I don't really know why I bothered to go since I never seemed to score, but perhaps I went because I'd spent nearly twelve quid on lessons at Eddie McEwan's Dancing Academy, and twelve quid meant something in those days; and although I say it myself I was pretty good at the fish tail, and with a bit of practice I could have got through a running six, but even so outside McEwan's Dancing Academy I never seemed to get any partners – I wasn't brash or pushy like some of the yobbos. I usually spent the evening standing with the lads looking slightly aloof, but it didn't seem to get me anywhere. I reckoned that in a year I'd only had a few Paul Joneses and about eight last waltzes, and six of those were with Hat.

I remember that at this particular dance I'd had a few jars and felt pretty sharp – I had a real natty sports jacket on with a pleat up the back, and a blue spotted clip-on bow tie – I looked just like one of the sophomores in American college films. Anyway as the music struck up the Paul Jones I stepped forward and joined the lads going round in a circle, but when the music stopped the girl I was facing said 'Just my luck' and sat down. I mean who was she expecting? Clark Gable? It wasn't as if she was a raving beauty – she had thick pebble glasses and a club foot. Before I could sidle off the floor a couple spun round and caught me right in the back, and my bow tie flew off its stud; as I bent down to pick it up my braces went, so that was me finished for the evening and I left rather sharpish to catch the last bus home.

Luckily as I turned into Market Street there it was, still at the terminus. All the seats were taken, and I had to stand; I didn't mind even though I'd been on my feet all night. There weren't many drunks so it was pretty quiet, and I stood there patiently in a cloud of fish and chips, beer and cheap scent. Bang on ten past eleven the driver climbed in his cab and started up; I waited for the 'ding, ding' but nothing happened. I saw the driver in the little square window looking back and then the conductress spoke:

'All right,' she said. 'I want one of you off.'

All the heads went round to have a look at her, then we looked at each other, then everybody turned back to the starting position, all staring sightlessly at the front. But the quiet resignation had gone and the atmosphere was electric – a herd of wildebeest sensing the approach of lions.

'Come on,' said the voice again. 'I'm only allowed eight standing and there's nine of you, so I want one of you off.'

All of us standing looked at each other, then turned to the front again, because now we were trying to avoid the hostile stares of those who were sitting down. The driver switched off and we heard him slam the door of his cab as he came round the back. He climbed aboard and stood by the conductress; he was a small chap, only coming up to his mate's ticket machine.

'What's happening, Elsie?' he said.

'There's nine standing, and the rules say there should only be eight.'

'Well, that's it then, isn't it?' he said.

'We don't make the rules.'

A voice piped up from somewhere: 'But it's the last bus.'

'I don't care if it's the last day on earth, I want one of you off.' The conductress folded her arms; she looked like a Japanese wrestler asking for all-comers.

The driver lit the stub of a fag, and said, 'We should have left five minutes ago. I don't mind, I get paid for this.'

Nobody moved and there was a hush. Then somebody upstairs started singing 'Why are we waiting?' but nobody joined in, so it died a natural death.

'That's it, then,' said the conductress. 'You've had your chance, we're going for the police,' and they stepped down. All of us standing looked uncomfortably at each other. I honestly didn't know if I was last on, because about five of us got on together, but I certainly wasn't about to get off and walk eight miles home. It was now twenty past, and I was nervous; as I held the strap a trickle of cold sweat ran from my armpit.

Just then there was a scuffle and a little man loaded with parcels swung himself on to the bus. 'Just made it,' he wheezed. 'I thought I'd missed it.' He stood next to me and he could hardly get his breath. 'He's late tonight, isn't he?' he gasped, but nobody answered him.

Everybody tensed and tried to see out. A large policeman was approaching, followed by the bus crew. The policeman stood on the platform and surveyed us.

'All right,' he said. 'You're all acting like a bunch of kids. We can't have this bus stuck here all night, some of you want to get home. One of you got on last and whoever it is gets off.' His gaze wandered over the standing crowd. 'I'll ask you once more,' he said. 'Who was the last to get on?'

The old man gazed up at him like a spaniel who's just wet the carpet. 'I suppose I was,' he said.

'Well, then,' said the large policeman. 'Get off.'

The old man collected his parcels and stepped back on to the kerb. The policeman stepped down with him and the conductress took her place with a look of triumph. 'There you are, you see,' she said. 'If you'd been sensible in the first place some of you would have been home now.'

Well, what with the release of tension I think somebody sniggered, then somebody else chuckled, and before the driver was comfortable in his cab the bus was rocking with laughter. The conductress looked from one to the other, her eyes wild.

'Stop it,' she said. 'Stop it. Shut your faces.' But the more she shouted the more hysterical was the laughter.

The conductress was by now in tears and the driver dashed round again. 'What's the matter now?' he said.

The conductress collapsed on the stairs, tears streaming down her face. 'They're all laughing at me,' she cried hysterically. 'Shut your stupid faces.'

The driver put his arm round her shoulders and helped her from the bus. As he led her back into the terminus he could still hear the laughter.

'What's up?' said the inspector.

'I don't know,' said the driver, 'but Elsie's in no condition to take this bus out.'

The inspector looked at her. She was sobbing fit to bust, and one of her stockings was hanging down. 'All right,' he said. 'Jessie hasn't gone home yet. I'll see if she'll take it.'

And so Jessie climbed aboard the bus. By this time we'd all sobered up, and were in fairly good order. Jessie was just reaching up to ding the bell when she caught sight of the little old man standing forlornly on the pavement clutching his parcels.

'What's up with you, grandad?' she said.

'I want to go to Shaw Road end,' he said.

'Well, get on then. We're going now.'

And with that she helped him up, ding dinged the bell,

and off we set. A great cheer, went up and we sang all the way, Jessie too. Whenever anybody got off we all said 'Goodnight'. I could have gone round the world on that last bus. There was more Christianity in the air that Saturday night than in all the churches on the following morning.

'It's not Tillie Truelove, it's the lighthouse.'

THE LAST TIME I SAW BOGSEA

Every year my sister and I spend a week's holiday in Bogsea. Its not the greatest watering hole in the western hemisphere, but it's on the coast, and apart from the east wind, and the fairly constant rainfall it's quite pleasant if you wrap up well.

We neither like it nor dislike it. It's become a habit, and we know our way around, which is important – for instance you can spot the first-timers; when they're turfed out of their digs after breakfast if it's fine they're OK, but more often than not when it's raining they waste the whole morning scurrying about looking for somewhere to keep dry. Hat and I, being regulars, know the ropes now; if it's raining, no messing about – straight out of the front door, across the road and into the bus shelter. It's not quite as warm as Marks and Spencer's, but it's a whole lot cheaper.

We always stay at Mrs Webb's boarding house. The food's good and there's plenty of it if you like cabbage, and being regulars we get certain perks. We have a very good table in the dining-room for instance, also, if the weather is very bad we're allowed to stay indoors with use of the ludo and draughts, and of course we're like one of the family now – Mrs Webb calls us Eric and Hattie, and we call her Mrs Webb. This year before we left on our annual pilgrimage we went through the checklist as usual: milk cancelled, papers cancelled, gas off and an out-of-order sign on the bell to fool casual burglars.

We caught the usual train to Bogsea at Victoria. Everything was normal except for one big difference – we had Mr Brown and Corky with us. I was dead against it from the start. I told Hat that we see Mr Brown and Corky practically every day of our lives, and the idea of going to Bogsea is to get away from them for a week. I mean I can understand Hat wanting Mr Brown along; she could visualize herself showing him round the place, taking him to the novelty gift shop, collecting shells on the beach for him to take home and perhaps be reminded of her every time he took one out to polish it . . . but Corky – that was something else. I told her that the reason we'd always been able to relax at Bogsea was that Corky was keeping an eye on our house, but Hat said that was precisely why we were taking him. The last time we'd left him in charge the place was a shambles when we got back. Empty bean cans, furniture all over the place. Corky pleaded ignorance and said it had been very windy, which I couldn't quite figure out, but under pressure he admitted he'd had a couple of friends round. Hat picked up a pair of corsets and said: 'What kind of friends?'

Corky gulped and said: 'That pair of corsets belonged to Harry Pangbourne. He had to wear 'em because he had a bad back.'

Straightaway Hat snapped: 'He had a bad front as well,' and threw a bra in Corky's face. The only reason she didn't prefer charges was that we got quite a bit of loot on the empties.

So this year Hat decided it was safer to bring Corky with us.

Anyway the journey down to Bogsea was the longest it had ever been. Apart from the fact that we were two hours late Mr Brown was at his condescending best. 'First time I've travelled second, quite comfortable really,' and 'When is the first sitting for lunch?' Hat coughed apologetically and I explained it didn't have a dining-car; we were only going to Bogsea and it was not the midnight train to Istanbul. That shut him up. Corky didn't care; he'd brought a stack of food with him and ate steadily throughout the journey. I'll bet he had more provisions with him than they had in the buffet car. Hat tried to liven things up with 'I spy with my little eye', but Mr Brown snorted and looked out of the window, so that was the end of that. By the time we got off the train I was already homesick, and you know what a crummy place we live in.

Unfortunately we had to walk from the station because it was just starting to drizzle, and taxi drivers don't like hanging about in the rain. Mr Brown was moaning all the way. I didn't see why he should be so upset at having to walk – after all I was carrying one of his suitcases, and Hat was carrying his other two as well as ours. It was a pitiful procession: me leading because I knew the way; then Corky, holding a parcel over his head; then Mr Brown with the one umbrella; and a furlong behind came Hat, loaded down like a bundle of sherpas. Suddenly the heavens opened, and it poured.

Straightaway I was in the bus shelter, hustled by Corky. Mr Brown took his time, because after all he had the umbrella; then we watched as Hat struggled the last few yards. Gone was the Margaret Thatcher bouffant golden hairstyle she set out with – three hours at the hairdresser's and now in five minutes she looked like a cold suet pudding with custard. We stood in a miserable line watching the rain belt down. Corky looked out of the side window and there was a poster glistening in the rain with the top corner peeling off. It showed a dolly bird lying on the beach with the sun beaming down, and underneath it said 'Come to sunny Bogsea.'

Corky sniffed. 'The bloke who painted that wants locking up.'

Hat quickly took up the cudgels. 'It's not always like this. We've had some marvellous summers here, haven't we, Eric?'

I blew a raindrop off the end of my nose. 'Oh yes,' I said. 'What about that Wednesday in 1952?'

'Oh come on, Eric. Look at the year before last – the sun was so strong you had to buy a hat.'

'Nothing to do with the weather though was it? It was on account of the seagulls.'

Mr Brown's lip curled. 'Very funny,' he said. 'Trust you to start the holiday with a coarse remark. Do you know any more jokes like that?'

I looked him straight in the eye. 'As a matter of fact I do. If you want seagull stories, I've got a million of 'em.'

Hat straightened up from wiping Mr Brown's suitcases with her hankie. 'Eric!'

'It's OK, Hat, it's the one about the man selling seagulls. You know – ', and I whispered it to her.

'Oh yes, that one. Oh, it's funny this one, Mr Brown. There's this man on the beach selling seagulls, you see, and – '

I stepped in before she could ruin the joke. 'Hang on,' I said. 'I'll tell it. He asked me.'

Hat just giggled, so I turned to Mr Brown. 'There's this man selling seagulls, you see. He's on the beach shouting "Seagulls one pound each – get your lovely seagulls here, one pound each".'

Mr Brown broke in: 'Just get on with it, Sykes. We don't require all the character voices.'

'OK,' I said. 'Anyway he's selling these seagulls for one pound each, and a bloke came up to him, gave him a pound and said "I'll have one". "Right", says the man, and put the pound in his pocket, and goes on shouting "Seagulls one pound each." The fellow who gave him a pound said "Hang on, where's my seagull?" And the man pointed to one flying past and said, "There's your one." '

Well, Hat fell about laughing, and I was a bit chuffed because I'd told it well, and even Corky was smiling, but Mr Brown was looking at each of us in amazement.

'Why on earth did he want a seagull?'

Corky shook his head sadly. 'Don't you get it, Charlie. It's a joke – "There's your one", and the man has to try and catch it.' Then he laughed as if he'd told the joke.

I looked at Mr Brown. 'Get it?'

Mr Brown's forehead puckered up in concentration. 'What I don't understand is, why did he want a seagull in the first place? It isn't as if they're edible.'

He looked at Corky for support, but Corky shook his head sadly and leaned across him to me. 'The penny hasn't dropped yet.'

The ran had now eased off, and Mr Brown stepped out of the shelter to shake his umbrella. But Corky hadn't finished with him; he tapped him on the arm and, as if speaking to a child, he said: 'You see, Charlie, there's this man on the beach, and he had a lot of seagulls for sale.'

Hat broke in: 'Well, they're not his, actually.'

Corky stopped dead in his tracks and turned to Hat. 'And he's selling them?'

Hat wished she hadn't said anything but she tried to pass it off. 'Well, yes. But seagulls are seagulls – I mean they belong to anybody, don't they?'

Corky squared his shoulders and put on his policeman's face. 'They do *not* belong to anybody, madam. They're crown property.'

By this time I was getting cold, and wishing I'd never started it, so I picked up my bag and said, 'It's only a joke.'

Corky looked at me gravely. 'It's against the law.'

'Oh, for goodness sake, Corky. You're on holiday, just forget you're a policeman for one week.'

'Never mind that, lad,' he said. 'If I catch him selling seagulls, he'll be inside so fast his feet won't touch the promenade.'

Hat shook her head ruefully. 'Don't tell any more jokes, Eric.'

Mr Brown turned his head. 'I second that, and before I die of pneumonia can you tell me when this bus is due?'

I looked at Hat, then at him. 'What bus?'

Mr Brown clucked in exasperation. 'The bus to take us wherever this lodging house is.'

'We don't need a bus. It's right there across the road – Mon Repos.'

Mr Brown's voice went up an octave: 'Well, for pete's sake why are we standing here in this freezing cold, like a bunch of wet nanas?'

'It's your fault,' I said. 'You asked me if I had any more jokes like that and I told you one.'

'That's right,' chirped Hat. 'You did ask him, Mr Brown.'

'Yes, I know I did, but I didn't think he was going to tell one, did I.'

Corky slapped him on the back. 'Oh, come on, Charlie. We're on holiday. Where's your sense of humour? Smile . . . let's all have some fun.'

Mr Brown wasn't so easily consoled. 'You can have some fun if you wish,' he snapped. 'You can pedal up and down the prom on a unicycle whistling the Marseillaise for all I care, but I intend to get indoors for a large whisky and a hot bath.' He prepared to cross the road.

Hat restrained him. 'Mrs Webb doesn't allow alcohol in the house.'

Mr Brown's face fell. 'Oh, for goodness sake,' he said. 'Well, I'll just have to make do with a hot bath.'

This time I stopped him. 'What time is it?'

Mr Brown glanced at his watch: 'Twenty past twelve.'

'Oh, what a pity,' I said. 'You've missed it by five minutes.'

Mr Brown looked helplessly from me to Hat. 'I can't even have a bath?'

'It's not the Ritz Carlton, you know.'

'I knew it,' he said. 'It's going to be a disaster. I don't know why I let you talk me into coming here in the first place.'

Well, I wasn't letting him get away with that. 'Me talk you into it? You practically begged to come with us. "I'm sick of the Bahamas", you said.'

Corky snorted. 'The Bahamas? He's never set foot in the Bahamas.'

'Oh really, constable. It's not necessary to go to a place to be sick of it.' And with that he stepped into the road, narrowly missing the horse-drawn tram.

We were about to follow when Corky stopped us. 'Hang on a second,' he said, and we saw a young policeman approaching.

'Now what?' I said.

Out of the corner of her mouth Hat whispered: 'Think he wants to report the man selling seagulls.'

Corky approached the young constable, and gave him a perfunctory salute. 'Morning, constable. Everything all right?'

The young policeman looked at us in turn, then leaned forward slightly towards Corky to see if he could detect the smell of alcohol. Satisfied, he stepped back a pace. 'Yes, sir. Can I help you?'

Corky beamed at him. 'No, no, lad. But when you report in you might inform your superior that Turnbull's in town.'

Hat and I exchanged glances. The young PC's eyes narrowed. 'Turnbull?'

Corky took out his identification card. 'Constable Turnbull F Division East Acton. If you need any assistance while I'm down here I'll be at Mon Repos,' and he winked.

The young PC smiled. 'Oh, I get you. Thanks very much. I'll let the sergeant know, and if a spate of murders breaks out we'll be round for you like a shot.'

I looked at the young PC. 'Murder?' I said. 'He's not exactly head of the CID. He specializes in stray dogs.'

The young PC smiled. 'Ah well, then. I'll see what I can do – we'll let a few of them loose and he can round 'em up.'

Corky tapped the PC's chest: 'Listen, sonny, when I was your age I was in the Flying Squad. Oh yes, when the East End of London was known as Hell's Kitchen. There was one particular time – '

The policeman started to move off. Corky held his arm 'Look at me when I'm talking!'

Hat picked up the suitcases. 'We're going to get the Siege of Sidney Street again. I'm off.'

'So am I,' I said. 'Otherwise we'll miss lunch.'

That was it. At the mention of lunch Corky's eyes glazed over and he picked up his brown paper parcel. He turned to the policeman: 'Aye well, lad, bear it in mind – Turnbull. And if I can be of any assistance don't hesitate to let me know.'

The young constable came to attention and saluted. 'Thank you, sir. The chief will be easier in his mind now he knows you're here.'

The sarcasm was lost on Corky, who just nodded. 'All right lad, carry on.'

As the young constable watched us struggle up the steps of Mon Repos he rubbed his chin thoughtfully and contemplated three things: (a) they were so worked to death in London that Constable Turnbull was old before his time; (b) he was in disguise; and (c) that ID card had been out of date since about 1965. He turned away and strolled down the prom, hoping to spot a stray nude.

Now one thing about Mrs Webb's boarding house is that it's run on strict lines, and one or two of our prisons should take a leaf out of her book. As we stood nervously in the hallway among the coats and umbrellas and buckets and spades, Hat and I knew we were off on the wrong foot. We were late. Corky was already rubbing his hands together as the smell of lunch hung heavy on the damp air.

'Right,' he said. 'Which is the dining-room?'

I was standing with my ear pressed to the door. Hat mouthed: 'Have they started?' and made the motion of using a knife and fork. I shrugged and Hat pushed me aside and listened. 'It's all right,' she whispered. 'She's reading the regulations.'

'Oh,' I said. 'Shall we go in, or shall we wait till she's finished?'

Hat looked at her watch, but the decision was made. Corky, unable to resist the smell of food, boldly opened the door and entered. He looked round, nodded at the room in general, and was joined by Mr Brown. Hat and I followed, trying to look as inconspicuous as possible.

Mrs Webb's eyes followed us over the rim of her pince-nez, and she looked pointedly at her watch. I smiled weakly but she pursed her lips and returned to the regulations. 'Rule 37,' she said. 'No ladies in gentlemen's rooms, unless married. Rule 38. All boarders will be in by eleven sharp, and lastly all boarders must vacate the hotel by 9.30 each morning and return at 12 noon for lunch unless I have been notified to the contrary in writing twenty-four hours previously. Now is that clear?'

She looked round the room. There was a general murmur of assent, then Mr Brown coughed to gain her attention and spoke up.

'Mrs Webb.'

'Well?'

'Er, Mrs Webb, with regard to the bathrooms – '

She held up her hand. 'You may use it freely, except when the weather is fine – then I prefer you to go down the yard.'

Mr Brown looked at me perplexed for a moment. Then he turned to Mrs Webb and smiled: 'No, no. You misunderstand me – for a bath,'

Mrs Webb's eyebrows went up a notch. 'A bath,' she said. 'What day will you require one?'

Mr Brown looked at me again, but I pretended to be examining the cutlery. He turned to Mrs Webb. 'Well, every day, naturally.'

At this all the heads swivelled round to look at him. Mrs Webb, unperturbed, was writing on her clipboard: 'Room 14 every day.' Then she looked up. 'You'll find the bathroom available from 6 am to 6.15. You follow Captain Thompson.' And with that she swept out of the room.

Mr Brown swung round towards us and hissed: 'This is intolerable, Sykes. Can't even have a bath when I want one.'

'Don't look at me,' I said. 'You should have had one before you left home.'

Hat leaned forward. 'In any case, Mr Brown, that geyser in the bathroom is a bit suspect. When you turn the hot on get back against the wall. If it rumbles nicely you'll be quite safe, but if it starts shaking and clanging get behind the wash basin, or the best thing of all is to stand on the fire escape and reach in through the window and turn it off.'

The look on Mr Brown's face was worth a couple of quid, but I knew Hat was laying it on a bit thick. 'Come on, Hat. It's not as bad as that.'

'How do you know?' she said. 'You've never used it.'

Corky chuckled. 'I'd give anything to see Charlie here on the fire escape with his bare – '

Hat banged the table. 'Please, constable,' she said. 'You're not down at the station now.' Then she looked across at Mr Brown, who was a picture of abject misery, and the mother in her came to the fore. 'Cheer up, Mr Brown. It's not as black as it's painted – for instance, here you are on table number six with us.'

Mr Brown shrugged. 'What's so special about table number six?'

'Ah well, you see, it's your first visit. The new ones have to sit over there in the corner where there's a draught and you can always smell cabbage. Then over the years you move up towards the window – that's the plum table. You can watch the traffic while you eat, and see the little table over there under the aspidistra.' She pointed discreetly, and Mr Brown looked at it with distaste.

'Well, we were on that table four years running, weren't we, Eric?'

I shuddered.

Mr Brown shrugged. 'It looks perfectly all right to me.'

I beckoned him closer. 'It *looks* all right,' I said, 'but things used to drop out of the aspidistra.'

Mr Brown looked quickly across to the plant.

'You'd be getting stuck into the soup – you look away for a second and *plop*.' When I said 'plop' Mr Brown jerked back and gulped noisily. I went on: 'All right if it was clear soup, but with brown windsor you could never be sure.'

Mr Brown paled and his eyes widened. Even Corky frowned, and if he was hungry he would have drunk a bowlful of the Limpopo.

Hat slapped me playfully, then addressed Mr Brown: 'He's having you on, Mr Brown.'

'I didn't think for a moment he was serious,' he said sternly; but during the week that followed he never passed that plant without holding a hankie to his mouth.

'Anyway,' said Hat, carrying on where she had left off, 'we were at that table for four years running.'

I nodded. 'Four years, and we'd have been there yet if Mr Bottomley hadn't fallen off the pier.'

Hat kicked me under the table and I realized that the other boarders were listening. Mr Bottomley's body had never been found, and the boarding house was always rife with speculation. Some boarders thought he'd run off with Mrs Webb's maid; others that Mrs Webb fancied him and that both Mr Bottomley and her maid were buried somewhere on the beach. But whatever the solution Mr Bottomley's name was taboo at Mon Repos and more than one boarder foolish enough to broach the subject had been sent packing the same day, and no refund either.

Luckily the tension was broken as Mrs Webb poked her head round the door; she was smiling at me. Well, it's hardly a smile – it's as if she has her foot in a bear trap and she doesn't want anyone to know. She beckoned me and disappeared again.

Hat grabbed my wrist. 'Do you think she heard?'

'No, of course not. This happens every year.'

I looked round the room, then leaned across the table. 'Every year she tries to mark my card.'

Mr Brown affected indifference. 'She does what?'

'Mrs Webb. She finds me a nice girl with a view to matrimony.'

Mr Brown snorted and I was about to elucidate when Mrs Webb looked in again.

'OK, Mrs Webb. I'm coming,' and I followed her into the kitchen.

Corky nudged Mr Brown. 'You know, Charlie, it's time you found a wife and settled down.'

Mr Brown was horrified. 'Me?' he said.

Corky turned to Hat. 'Is there a Mr Webb?'

Hat shook her head. 'No, she's a widow.'

Corky stared at Mr Brown. 'You know, Charlie, I think your ship's come in. From what Hattie tells me she's a marvellous cook. It's a nice going concern here, and you could have a bath every day.'

Mr Brown glared at him. 'Me and Mrs Webb? What a horrid thought! And in any case if I ever did consider marriage I certainly wouldn't be a widow's second husband.'

Hat patted his arm. 'It's better than being her first,' she said, and she nearly fell over backwards laughing.

That's when I returned with this girl, Mrs Webb's latest protégé for the marriage stakes. I mean the last year's filly was a non-starter, but this one would have found it hard going to parade round the paddock. To call her hair mousy would have sent the mice dashing off to the Race Relations board. She wore thick pebble glasses – or they may have been cracked – and she was much too thin.

I walked her to the table and introduced her. 'This is Miss Palethorpe. My sister Hat, Constable Turnbull and Mr Brown.'

She smiled awkwardly at everybody, and I coughed discreetly, hoping she'd go, but instead she sat down in my chair. Mr Brown looked up at me and chuckled. I looked across to the window and said: 'It's clearing up a bit.' Everybody looked out. Then once more it went quiet and I was still standing there like a pork chop at a vegetarian convention, but before I took root Mrs Webb bustled in with a chair, and I smiled my relief as I sat down.

Mrs Webb chucked my cheek and whispered: 'Don't be shy, her name's Jocelyn.' Then she clapped her hands and the maids came round with the brown windsor.

Normally the food at Mrs Webb's is one of the highlights of the holiday, but that first meal was a disaster. I could feel everybody's eyes on me and Jocelyn. Once we reached for the pepper at the same time and our hands touched.

'I'm sorry,' I blurted, and as I went to hand it to her the top came off. She sneezed and her glasses fell into her soup. I immediately reached for my napkin to wipe them; unfortunately it wasn't my napkin but the tablecloth, and I dragged my soup into my lap. Luckily there wasn't much left in my bowl, but as I took my fork to scratch out the stain I dropped it. When I bent down to pick it up Jocelyn had the same idea, and *wallop* – the crack of our heads made Mrs Webb look in from the kitchen.

I couldn't excuse myself and go to my room, because nobody leaves the table at Mrs Webb's before the meal is finished without a doctor's certificate. But eventually the pudding was cleared away, and Corky said it was the best meal he'd ever had, especially the cabaret. Even Mr Brown was so amused by watching me and Jocelyn that he never sent anything back to the kitchen.

Jocelyn had got round to calling me Ricky, and Mr Brown leaned over to me and said: 'That's your week taken care of, Ricky.'

I was just about to tell them all to take a running jump when Mrs Webb walked in with a pile of local newspapers, and I remembered that this was the annual ritual of 'Find the Lady'. Mrs Webb placed a paper on every table, then she came to us and pointed to the picture.

'That's her this year,' she said, 'Her name is Tillie Truelove.'

I looked at the side view of a blonde girl, but she wasn't very recognizable.

'It gets tougher every year,' I said. 'Look at that picture – you can only see part of her nose.'

Hat leaned across. 'Well, at least we know she's blonde.'

Mrs Webb sniffed. 'It's time you won it. You've been trying long enough.'

Corky glanced at the photo. 'What is it, a competition or something?'

Mrs Webb looked at him as if he was a foreigner. 'Oh, I forgot. You're new, aren't you? Oh well, you're in for a very hectic week, isn't he, Eric?'

I nodded with a sickly smile, because Joycelyn's knee was pressed so hard against mine that I feared for my cartilage.

Corky looked at Mrs Webb. 'Well, what happens?'

She tapped the newspaper. 'The rules are all there. You see, every day this girl is in a certain area at a given time – see, it tells you where underneath. Well then, all you have to do is spot her, then you say – ' Mrs Webb lifted her pince-nez and read: 'You are Tillie Truelove. I read the *Daily Bugle* regularly and I claim the five pounds.'

Mr Brown's lip curled.

'Is that all you have to do?' said Corky.

'Ah yes, but you have to be carrying a copy of the paper with you. And if you're right she hands over a fiver.'

Mr Brown fitted a cigeratte to his holder. 'Sounds rather facile to me.'

Mrs Webb glanced at him sharply. 'It passes the time, doesn't it? You ask young Eric here.'

Corky chuckled. 'Young Eric?'

I squirmed with embarrassment. Why did she have to keep calling me 'young Eric' in front of people? I'm not all that young. Hat says it's the way I behave, which is ludicrous – just because I happen to like donkey rides, and what if I do sometimes wear a cowboy hat? Good grief, it's only made of paper, and we are supposed to be on holiday enjoying ourselves.

'Isn't that right, Eric?'

I jerked out of my reverie. 'Sorry, Mrs Webb.'

Mrs Webb folded her arms. 'I said you've been searching for her every time for at least twelve years, haven't you?'

'Any luck?' said Corky.

Hat broke in: 'He's never actually won the fiver, but he's had umpteen dates, been arrested twice, and had his face slapped several times.'

Corky leaned back in his chair. 'I begin to see now why you invited me down here,' he said.

Hat and I looked at each other. In the first place we hadn't invited him, as he put it. As far as I could see he'd just tagged along without so much as a by your leave; and secondly an invitation seemed to imply that he was our guest, and I hoped he wasn't expecting us to pick up his bill. I decided to step on it right away.

'It's the first I've heard of inviting you,' I said. 'When you came to the station with us I thought it was just to wave us off. I didn't know you were actually coming with us.'

Hat put her hand on my arm. 'I did make the reservation for him,' she said.

'Yes, but that doesn't mean we've adopted him. He pays for his own holiday.'

Corky tapped the table with his finger. 'It's lucky for you, my lad, that I am here though, isn't it, with this newspaper competition of yours.'

'What are you talking about?' I said.

Corky's eyes glinted. 'It stands to reason. Oh yes, I'm highly trained for this sort of work. With my background I'll have her challenged in no time.'

'Oh, really,' I exclaimed. 'It's not that simple, mate. I know – I've been at it for twelve years. "You are Doris Pureheart . . . you are Sue Sweety . . . you are Alice Heartthrob". If anybody's trained for it, it's me.'

Corky smirked. 'Trained for it? Twelve years and you haven't copped once – and they even tell you in the paper where's she's going to be and at what time! Good grief, if we lads in the force had the same record as you Dr Crippen'd still be running around today.'

Hat laughed and tried to change the conversation, but I wasn't letting Corky come out on top.

'All right, Mr Constable Sherlock Holmes, if you're so certain I'll have a little bet with you. Never mind the five pounds you win, I'll give another five pounds for every time you spot Tillie Truelove. Mind you, if you don't spot her you pay *me* five pounds.'

Hat shot me a warning glance.

'It's OK, Hat, no problems. He couldn't spot her if she was fifteen foot tall with bells going and a light flashing on her head.'

Corky looked at me quizzically. 'Every time I spot her and claim the fiver you will also give me a fiver.'

'That's right,' I said. 'But she's in about six different locations at different times, and if you don't spot her once you owe me thirty quid.'

Corky grabbed the newspaper and stared hard at the photo, then he sat back. 'Done – it's a bet.'

Hat dabbed at her nose with a hankie. 'Well, that's it, then. That's our holiday money gone.'

'Course it isn't. Listen, Hat. This way I don't even have to waste time looking for her. Every day he comes in and gives me thirty quid.'

Jocelyn touched my knee again. 'That'll give us more time together, Ricky.'

Mrs Webb smiled fondly at us both and I knew in my bones this was going to be the worst holiday I'd ever had, and I've had some crummy ones.

Being our first day, we were allowed to stay indoors after lunch in order to unpack, so at least I could have a little privacy in my room. Usually I hung my stuff up, then memorized the words, 'You are Tillie Truelove, I read the *Daily Bugle* regularly, and I claim the five pounds.' It doesn't sound much, but I'd heard that if you got one word out of place when you challenged her you weren't entitled to the fiver, and it would be stupid to pick her out, then lose the money on a technicality.

However I was just unwrapping my plimsolls when there was a knock on the door. I froze, then there was another knock and the door handle rattled. 'Eric, are you in there?'

Thank goodness, it was only Hat. I let her in. 'Why did you lock the door?'

'I thought it might be Jocelyn.'

Hat snorted. 'I don't think she's that hard up.'

'Oh no? You should have seen what she was doing to my leg under the table. I'm surprised I don't walk with a permanent limp.'

Hat raised an eyebrow.

'Oh, come on, Hat. I know I'm not Clint Eastwood, but if I want a girl I'll go and get one, so why does Mrs Webb do it? Every year the same – she always throws a girl at me. You'd think she was running a marriage bureau.'

'Oh, she doesn't mean any harm. She probably thinks its time you settled down. Anyway, forget it. Put your coat on.'

I looked at her. 'Where are we going?'

Her face lit up. 'We're on holiday. We're in Bogsea. I thought we might have a stroll down to the lifeboat house.'

'Hallelujah', I said. 'The lifeboat house. Every year we walk down to the lifeboat house, put 10p in the box, then back to the digs.'

Hat was unabashed. 'All right then, we'll go down to the novelty gift shop.'

'We're not going down to the novelty gift shop either. We've got more plastic shells at home with "Bogsea" on 'em than they'll ever have.'

Hat waved her arms about. 'Well, we don't have to go to the novelty gift shop. We can – well, we can walk right past it.' She started twiddling one of the brass knobs on the bedstead, then she smiled. 'Why don't we go to the beach?'

'In this weather?'

That seemed to be the whole gamut of Bogsea. Hat made for the door. 'I'll go and find out what's on at the pictures.'

'You do that,' I said, and sat on the bed. The pictures – that was a laugh. Last time we went it was *Lives of a Bengal Lancer* – well, it was until the film broke. What a way to spend a holiday – leave a comfortable home and travel forty-odd miles to walk round a lifeboat house. Every year the same: we migrate like a flock of drunken starlings, and I was heartily sick of it. Sick of these digs, sick of Mrs Webb and her annual wedding fodder, sick of the view from my window – another boarding house. I got up, walked to the window, and gazed idly across at Dunrovin. My eye caught a movement in one of the windows and suddenly the adrenalin hit me. There was a gorgeous blonde in just bra and pants and she appeared to be unpacking. Like a flash of sunlight through the clouds I knew it. It had to be. It was Tillie Truelove. I rushed to my suitcase, grabbed my binoculars, and had a good old shufti. Then I checked it with the picture in the newspaper – it was remarkable: she had the same hairstyle, and when she turned in a certain way it was without a doubt Tillie True-love.

I felt somebody at my elbow, and I turned to see Hat and Jocelyn looking over my shoulder.

'What is it this time, Eric?' asked Hat in a cold voice. 'A red-crested plover?'

'Eh? No, Hat. It's her. It's Tillie Truelove. Here, have a look.'

Hat ignored the binoculars and drew the curtain.

Jocelyn sighed. 'I wish I was blonde like her.'

'A walking goldmine over there,' I said. 'All Bogsea on the alert, and I know where she is before the contest even starts.'

Hat folded her arms. 'And what if she isn't Tillie True-love?'

'She's got to be, hasn't she – blond, good-looking? She wouldn't be on holiday in Bogsea, not a girl like that. She'd be in the south of France. So she's got to be here working, and even if it isn't Tillie Truelove it's going to be great chatting her up. "You are Tillie Truelove." "No, I'm not." "Oh, I thought you were." "Fancy a drink." "I'd love one." Bingo!'

Hat put her arm round Jocelyn's shoulders. 'He always talks like this, Jocelyn, but he doesn't mean anything.' She took hold of my arm. 'Come on, Eric. Jocelyn's going to take us up on the cliff.'

I shuddered. 'Sorry, Hat. I'd love to come but – er – I'd sooner get my unpacking finished.'

'You can look down at the sea and ships and things,' said Jocelyn.

'Some other time.'

Hat buttoned her coat. 'Well, we'll go, Jocelyn. I'm sure Eric won't mind us borrowing his binoculars.'

My face fell. 'Oh, for goodness sake. I might as well come with you.'

Hat smiled and opened the door. We were just in time to catch a glimpse of Mr Brown in his dressing-gown with a towel over his arm, stealing up the corridor on tiptoe. He jumped like a scalded cat when Hat called him.

'Mr Brown, you can't go for a bath in the afternoon. You know Mrs Webb's rules.'

Mr Brown looked over his shoulder, then whispered: 'Mrs Webb's gone to her room for a nap. She'll never know,' and he gleefully crept towards the bathroom.

Hat shook her head, saying: 'She'll know all right.'

Jocelyn looked alarmed. 'You won't tell on him, will you?'

I put my finger to my lip. 'Just wait,' I said, and sure enough five seconds later there was a rumbling, clanking, gurgling cacophony. Mr Brown shot by like the electric hare at White City, and Mrs Webb could be heard above it all asking who was responsible. Luckily as we got to the front door the rain started pelting down again, so I was able to go back to my room and cogitate.

Monday was day one of the Tillie Truelove operation. Corky was off early with his newspaper to case the South Esplanade, which was Tillie's first venue. My plan was not so complicated. I watched Tillie from my bedroom window, the idea being when she went I would follow. What could be simpler than that?

Mr Brown was casually pretending to read *The Times* in the bus shelter opposite the front door of the digs. He had overslept and missed his bathtime, but the minute Mrs Webb left to buy the daily provisions he intended to be in that tub like a shot. Poor old fool, I thought, little does he know that Mrs Webb always takes the plug with her.

Across the way I could see the blonde girl putting on her make-up. It was an hour yet before her first appearance on the esplanade, but I had to keep watch in case she went early, and it was no hardship although she was fully dressed – I must have missed that while I was having breakfast. Suddenly she grabbed a bag and made for the door. Straight-away I was downstairs, just in time to see her crossing the road to go to the beach. Once there she spread out her towel and slipped out of her dress – what a beauty – then came the ritual of the suntan lotion, even though the sun was weak. I figured the lotion was more for protection against the cold. I sauntered past her casually, then I sauntered back, then I skipped a couple of pebbles across the waves.

There was still half an hour before she had to go to work, so I decided to have a paddle. I wasn't over-keen, but taking my shoes and socks off would take some time, and I would be less conspicuous than standing there skimming pebbles out to sea; in any case my arm was getting tired. As I stepped into the water I glanced towards her out of the corner of my eye. She was talking to a well-built young man but, worse still, she was pointing at me. I looked round but there was no one else in sight, so it must have been me. I smiled and waved, and the man started walking towards me. He didn't look too friendly so I went slightly further into the sea, but he kept coming on and I struggled a little further out until the water was up to my knees. He stopped on the edge, and she came up and joined him.

'That's definitely the man that has been watching me through binoculars,' she said.

'Right,' he said, and started struggling with his belt.

There was nowhere for me to go except out, and I went. I'm not a bad swimmer, and I thought if I got far enough away he wouldn't follow me, but I was wrong, for he was already stripped and striding through the surf. I struck out for all I was worth, thrashing away in a mad panic towards America. After a few minutes I eased off. Gasping and retching I looked back: the beach seemed miles away, but there was the tiny figure of Tillie, and wading towards her was the big guy. He'd given up and I was safe.

After the first warm flood of relief panic struck me again – the beach was getting further away, and I realized that the tide was going out. I kicked my legs and tried to swim back but my strength had gone. I was being tossed about in the swell, and thinking what a stupid thing I'd done. I shouldn't have swum out to sea, I could have fallen down at his feet clutching my heart and saying, 'Where's my pills?' He wouldn't have dared touch me then. I thought about Hat, and a wave of remorse came over me. I thought if I ever got out of this I'd be kinder to her, perhaps take her a cup of tea on Sunday mornings. At one point I thought I heard a helicopter, but it was only my teeth chattering. I went to touch my nose but I couldn't feel anything at all. I thought I'd missed, and strangely enough I was past caring. The sea gently raised me up and I caught a glimpse of Bogsea, then down I went into a trough, up and down, up and down, and I began feeling drowsy. I felt I could float like this for ever. A seagull hovered above me, mewling and floating on the wind. I thought to myself, some poor sucker's paid a pound for that one. I never heard the boat engines approaching. I had already committed myself to the vast deep.

However, my number hadn't been called because when I opened my eyes I was in bed at Mrs Webb's. I noticed I was in my own room, but there was something different about it. Then I saw that there was a fire in the grate. It must have been late because the light was on, but there was something else – the window was boarded up. I thought about it: my watch said quarter past five, but that could have been either one of the quarter past fives in a day; and why board up the window? Then I remembered the blonde across the way. I decided it didn't really matter following Tillie anyway. All I had to do was lie back and collect thirty quid a day from Corky, who'd never spot her in a million years. I've known him walk right past his wife in an empty car park. Mind you, I don't blame him for that. Poor old Elsie – his eyes must have been bad when he married her; nobody could go off that much in forty years.

I quickly wiped her out of my mind and stared at the fire. It was a good fire. I hadn't had a fire in my bedroom since I fell asleep with a lighted cigarette – that was a narrow squeak, it could have been very nasty if the eider-down hadn't been damp. I began to take stock of the situation. The first thing was to find some excuse for floating outside the three-mile limit in flannels and a sports jacket. I fell off the pier – no, that wouldn't do, since there was a large wire fence to keep idiots like me from falling off. Perhaps I dived off the pier to save a drowning child? This idea appealed to me until I examined it. Where was the child now, and how had my shoes and socks come to be neatly lying on the beach a mile away? Then I thought of my shoes and socks and the blonde and the muscular young man. Of course they'd blown the gaff – it was probably them that had rescued me, then they'd brought me back here and told the whole story. Of course that was it, and that was why the window had been boarded up. I knew I'd never hear the last of it from Corky and Mr Brown.

Speaking of the devil the door opened, and he popped his head in. 'Ah, Sykes, so you're back in the land of the living,' he said, chuckling. 'We thought we'd lost you.'

Then Hat followed him in. 'Oh, you're awake. You had us all worried – the lifeboat, then the ambulance and crowds and everything.'

'The lifeboat?' I asked. 'The lifeboat came out for me?'

'Only just in time too,' said Mr Brown. 'The coxswain said another five minutes and it would have been too late.'

'The lifeboat,' I muttered and turned my head away. 'I call that ironic.'

Mr Brown and Hat looked at each other.

'What d'you mean "ironic", Eric?' Hat said.

I turned to her. 'For twelve years I've been coming

down here, and every year I walk round the lifeboat shed and religiously put 10p in the box. I've contributed pounds to that boat, and the only time in living memory it's put to sea I'm the only one who's missed it.'

Mr Brown raised one eyebrow. 'Luckily it didn't miss you, Sykes.'

Hat was indignant. 'You should be jolly grateful, Eric, to everybody for risking their lives to save you – the boat crew, the ambulance men, Mrs Webb put a fire in your room, Mr Brown here – '

I looked at her for a second. 'When did Mr Brown risk his life?'

'He didn't exactly risk his life, but he helped to save yours. He gave you a hot bath.'

I struggled to a sitting position. 'He did what?'

'When they carried you indoors he asked Mrs Webb to get a hot bath ready. Then he had them take you into the bathroom, then he gave you a hot bath, and lucky he did otherwise you might have got exposure.' I looked at Mr Brown and shuddered. I mean, I'm not a prude or anything like that; I didn't mind doctors seeing me with nothing on, or even a nurse if she's old enough – but Mr Brown, with no qualifications! Hat was exasperated. 'Well, at least you can say thank you.'

'Thank you,' I mumbled.

Mr Brown turned his head away, a little shamefaced, and I thought that was out of character. I was expecting him to come out with something like: 'Typical of your brother, you save his life and that's all the thanks you get.'

But here he was smiling weakly. 'It's only what anybody would have done,' he said, and in a flash I got the picture. They'd carried me into the bathroom, then he'd locked the door and nipped into the bath himself – luxuriating in a nice hot bath while I was stretched out stiff as a board on the floor.

I glanced sharply at him and he blushed, and I knew I'd hit on it. I'll bet he took a book in with him as well.

'I'll go and tell Mrs Webb you're awake,' said Hat. But as she spoke Mrs Webb, Jocelyn and Corky came in. They trotted out the usual platitudes.

Then, having ascertained that I was well enough, Mrs Webb said: 'I'll have to charge you extra for the fire and the electric light – ' she looked meaningly at the boarded window and sniffed. 'Then there's the bath.'

I looked at Mr Brown; he was nodding in agreement.

Then Corky leaned over the bed rail. 'Here's something else to cheer you up,' and he took out some fivers. 'What a day I've had,' he chuckled. 'Tillie Truelove: Esplanade 11 am, Winter Gardens 12 am. This afternoon 2.30 Floral Clock.' He held out the fivers. 'I spotted, challenged and collected at every location,' he beamed, 'so that's thirty quid you owe me.'

Hat looked at the ceiling in anguish. 'Thirty pounds, and there's still four days to go.' Then the dinner gong went and so did everybody else.

The following day I felt pretty chirpy, and I was about to get up when Jocelyn popped her head in. 'How do you feel today?' she said.

I just smiled bravely and shrugged, and she went on: 'If you're up to it you can come with me. I'll look after you.'

'Great,' I said, and made to get up, then pretended to slump back on the pillows as if exhausted.

She shook her head. 'You're not up to it yet, are you? Never mind. I'll be in every now and again to see if you want anything,' and thankfully she left.

So I was stuck with lying in bed bored to the back teeth, and because of the expense Hat had cancelled the fire, so I couldn't even look at that. But being here was marginally preferable to having to talk to Jocelyn, and besides that I had to think of a way of queering Corky's pitch – break his leg so he couldn't get out, or better still smash his glasses. But then knowing him and his knowledge of the National Health he'd probably have a dozen spare pairs on him and a boxful of false teeth. Since she'd brought my breakfast up I hadn't seen Hat, and of course Mr Brown was too embarrassed to face me.

I stared up at the light. Normally I wouldn't look directly at a lighted bulb, but Mrs Webb knew how to make a boarding house viable – it couldn't have been more than five watts. I thought about it idly, and decided that in all probability we were all being charged for 100 watts, so on lights alone she was making a 95 per cent profit. After a time I noticed that it was swinging slightly, so we were either in the middle of a slight earth tremor, or Mr Hackensmidt had somebody in his room. Then I decided it was a draught. My door was open and it was Jocelyn again. I groaned and turned my head away.

'You have a good rest,' she said, and I heard the door close behind her.

I wasn't so lucky the next time she came. I didn't hear her come in and she caught me trying to bore a hole in the boards covering the window, but she was a simple soul and believed me when I said I was merely trying to let a little light in.

'You poor thing,' she said, and I had to restrain her from taking the boards down altogether – I didn't want that much light, just enough to see whether Tillie was still there. As Jocelyn was about to leave she pointed to the boarded window and said: 'By the way, she went home this morning.'

At lunchtime Hat came in with a bowl of soup. I looked at it with complete apathy. 'What did you have for lunch?' I asked.

'Ooh, we had avocado pear with shrimp, lovely roast beef, Yorkshire pudding and cabbage.'

I held up my hand. 'Where's mine, then?' I said. 'I'm sick of this muck.'

'It's good for you. It'll build up your strength.'

'So will roast beef and Yorkshire pudding, but you can skip the cabbage.'

'I'm sorry, Eric, but I can't stop now. I have to go,' and she hurried to the door.

'Wait a minute, Hat.'

She stopped and turned. 'I'm late,' she said.

'Never mind that. We've paid for full board, and broth isn't full board. So if Mrs Webb's going to charge me for the bath, which whether I had one is questionable, and the fire – see that she makes a discount for the roast beef. OK?'

There was no answer, so I looked to the door and she wasn't there. She'd gone. Never even had the courtesy to say 'I'm off now.' I ate the broth reluctantly and was overwhelmed with self-pity. My one week's holiday – one miserable week, that's all – not a lot to ask to be able to enjoy the air and the beach and the novelty gift shop, and here I was bedridden, incapacitated, forcing down lukewarm broth, while everybody, even my own sister, was out enjoying themselves. All the year round at work I'm hale and hearty – just my luck to be struck down in my own time. On top of that I was thirty pounds in debt to Corky and the chances were that thirty pounds was only the tip of the iceberg.

I was right. At about six o'clock there was a smart rat-a-tat-tat on the door and Corky walked in, beaming. 'Evening, all,' he said. 'And how's the geriatric ward?'

I picked up the newspaper. 'Not now, Corky,' I said. 'I'm having a relapse.'

He sat on the bed. 'Don't be so soft. There's nothing wrong with you that a hard day's work won't cure.' He reached out for one of my sandwiches and I slapped his hand. 'I was only looking,' he said. 'And seeing as how your strength is coming back there's another thirty quid you owe me.'

I turned my head away, feigning indifference.

'Money for jam,' he chuckled, and I heard the door close. As he left I turned round, and would you believe it my sandwiches had gone and an apple. I was out of bed like a shot, I was going to get those sandwiches back if I had to hold him upside-down and shake 'em out. The door burst open just as I reached it, and I went flying back over the bed. It was Hat, breathless and so excited she didn't seem to notice I was getting up off the floor.

'Eric, oh Eric, I've got something to tell you.' Then she hurried to the door, and looked up and down the corridor to see if anyone was listening. 'Do you know what I did today?' she waited. It always exasperates me when Hat asks fatuous questions like that. How could I possibly know what she'd done apart from bringing me gruel at lunchtime, and belting me with the door? 'Listen, Eric,' she said. 'I followed Corky and I watched him challenging Tillie Truelove.'

'That's a big help, that is. Now he's got proof that he challenged Tillie.'

'Oh, no,' she went on. 'He didn't see me.'

A sudden thought struck me: 'You actually saw Tillie Truelove?'

'Yes,' said Hat, 'and saw her pay out the money.'

I looked at Hat in a new light. 'You know, Hat, I've underestimated you. You're a genius.'

She flushed with pleasure.

'Let's have it,' I said.

She looked puzzled. 'Have what?'

I made the money sign with finger and thumb, 'Thirty quid', then said: 'As soon as you saw Corky challenged, you waited till he'd gone, then you challenged her.'

Hat looked blank.

'You did see Tillie Truelove, didn't you?'

'Yes, I saw her all right. It was definitely Tillie Truelove. So what?'

I stared in disbelief. 'And you never challenged her and copped the fivers?'

Hat put her hand to her mouth. 'Oh dear,' she said. 'I never thought of that.'

I fell back on the pillows. It couldn't be true. It would be a kindness to have her put down.

She recovered herself and chuckled. 'That isn't what I wanted to tell you,' she said. 'I've found out how Corky does it.'

'You didn't follow him into the gents?'

'Of course not. I only . . . . ' Then she stopped, and blushed. 'Oh, Eric. Don't be so rude. I found out how he knows where Tillie Truelove is.'

I sat bolt upright.

She pulled a chair up to the bed and leaned forward. 'You know that young policeman we met on the first day?'

'Policeman?' I asked.

'In the bus shelter. Corky got chatting about the – '

I cut her off. 'Yes, I remember. What about him?'

'Well,' she said. 'His job is to keep an eye on Tillie Truelove, in case there's trouble.'

'What sort of trouble?'

'I dunno, Mrs Webb told me. She said somebody might think she was – well, that Tillie Truelove, well, was, being a girl and just hanging about, you know.'

'On the game,' I said.

'Yes.' She looked down. 'It's not easy being a woman. I mean if you're a man you can just stand there and nobody comes up and says "How much?" But if you're – '

Again I stopped her. 'Never mind Women's Lib, Hat. The young policeman who keeps an eye on her.'

'That's right,' she said. 'Well, all Corky had to do was look for him, don't you see – you can't miss a policeman in uniform – and when the young policeman stood near Tillie he took out his handkerchief and blew his nose. Then Corky knew it was Tillie.'

I thought for a moment. 'He could have a cold.'

'No,' she said. 'He blew it in all the different places that Tillie appeared and immediately Corky stepped up and challenged her.'

I stared at her in disbelief. No wonder he was so sure of winning – of all the crafty, low-down tricks to pull on a mate. I could feel my temper rising and I looked round the room for a weapon. 'I knew it,' I grated. 'I knew he was cheating somehow. He couldn't find her on his own – not Corky. He couldn't find a piano if it was tied to his leg.'

'Exactly,' said Hat. 'And that's where we've got him.'

'I'll have him all right,' I said, struggling to get out of bed.

'No, no. Listen,' she said, hardly able to contain herself. 'That young constable won't be on duty for a bit. He got knocked down by a taxi while he was directing traffic, and Mrs Webb says they're so short-staffed Tillie will be on her own the rest of the week.' She sat back, eyes shining, and a grin from ear to ear – and that opens up a lot of face.

I suddenly felt better. All right, he'd won on two days, but there were three left, and I knew Corky – underneath that carefully cultivated look of experienced reliability, intelligence and steadfastness he was useless; and what's more, tomorrow I would be in the hunt for Tillie. I was already thinking of how to tackle the problem.

On the following morning I asked Mr Brown, Hat and Jocelyn to my room after breakfast and I outlined my plan. On the bed was a map of Bogsea, and I'd ringed all the places where Tillie Truelove was to appear.

'Operation Find the Lady,' I said.

'Oh, not that stupid game,' said Mr Brown. 'Really, Sykes, if you're so hard up for five pounds why don't you ask me?'

'All right, then,' I said. 'Can I have five pounds?'

'Certainly not,' he replied indignantly, 'and if I'd known

that you'd asked me here in order to borrow money, I would never have come.'

Hat put her arm through his. 'Oh, come on, Mr Brown. It's just Eric's little joke, and he knows how we can spot Tillie.'

Mr Brown disengaged his arm. 'I'm sick of your brother's little jokes', he said. 'I had enough with the seagulls, and as for Tillie, I don't care if you spot her, stripe her or paint her all over in Dulux.'

'So you're not coming with us?' I said.

'No, I'm not. I have other things to do. Mrs Webb has to go to Clacton this morning.' Then he chuckled and took a bath plug out of his pocket. 'See you at lunch,' and he was gone.

'Well, there's only three of us now,' I said. 'That leaves a certain element of chance, but we might be lucky – now here is Tillie's first venue. The vicinity of the pier at eleven o'clock, right?'

They both nodded.

'OK so far. Now she may go on the pier or not, but that's easy. I'll watch the entrance – there's only one – so if she goes in or out I'll have her.'

Hat and Jocelyn looked at each other. 'Now to get to the pier vicinity you approach either from the South Promenade, or from the north. The only other way is across the road, in which case she'd have to go through the miniature golf, right?'

They both nodded again.

'So I'll be watching the pier in case she passes in or out of that. You, Jocelyn, will watch the North Promenade, and you, Hat, from the south. I was hoping that Mr Brown could have done the miniature golf, but that's a chance we'll have to take. Now is everything all clear?'

'What happens if one of us spots her?' said Hat.

'Challenge her, and if you're right we nip over and challenge her in turn. That's fifteen quid for a start. The other venues will be a piece of cake – we just follow her. OK?'

They stared down at the map for a few moments, deep in thought. Well, when I say deep in thought I was paying Hat a compliment – she was probably wondering how Mr Brown had got the hang of the boiler so quickly.

Jocelyn broke the silence. 'But wherever Tillie is there are always lots of people. If one of us spots her how will we contact the other two?'

I was waiting for that. I smiled. 'We'll each have a balloon.'

Hat looked at me quizzically. 'A balloon?'

'Yes, a balloon,' I said. 'There's a balloon man on the corner and he sells them.'

Hat laughed. 'You give him a pound and he lets one go. "Where's my one?" you say, and he points to it disappearing up in the air, and says "There you are",' and she laughed so much that I feared for her dress.

Jocelyn just looked on, perplexed.

'It's OK, Jocelyn. It's a private joke about seagulls,' I said, and waited till Hat was ready. She'd stopped laughing, but it takes some time for the rest of her to subside.

'Go on, Ricky,' said Jocelyn.

I winced. 'Well, we'll have three balloons, each on a six-foot piece of string, but we hold the balloons under our arm. Then when one of us spots Tillie whoever it is lets their balloon rise. The rest of us can't miss a balloon hovering six feet over the heads of the crowd.'

'What a good idea,' said Hat. 'Just like a marker buoy.'

'Exactly,' I said, and straightened up. The briefing was over.

Just as we left the digs we heard the clanking and thumping from upstairs, and as we stepped into the street I couldn't help laughing. There was Mr Brown on the fire escape, with a towel flapping round his thin, white legs, peering in through the bathroom window.

At a quarter to eleven we were in position. So far so

good, except that I felt such a fool holding a balloon under my arm, and whenever anybody looked at me strangely I said: 'You haven't seen a little boy, have you?' Pretending to have lost my little boy also gave me the excuse to search around for Tillie, then I had another piece of inspiration. I approached the lady selling tickets for the pier.

'You haven't seen a little boy, have you? He's with his mother, a blonde girl.'

The ticket lady shook her head. 'I haven't seen a little boy or a blonde girl. If I had I'd have challenged her. Tillie Truelove's round here somewhere.'

'Oh,' I said. 'Is she?' and wandered away.

I realized that it was going to be more difficult than I thought. The place was milling with people. There were one or two blondes, but I discounted them – one was pushing a pram while another was eating candy floss, and I didn't think Tillie would have done that. In any case they all carried copies of the *Daily Bugle*, so they were obviously looking as well. Then at about ten minutes past eleven the balloon went up literally and hovered six feet above the crowd, about fifty yards away. I was off like a shot, shoving and elbowing my way through till I got to the balloon. Hat was standing there, but her balloon was still under her arm, and she was staring at a little boy who was holding the balloon and staring back at her.

The little boy tugged my jacket, and said, 'Hey mister, would you like to hold this balloon?'

'No thanks, sonny,' I said. 'I've got one of my own.'

'It's not mine. A woman asked me to hold it for her, and I have to go now.'

Hat stepped forward. 'Was she a medium-sized, with glasses and brown hair?'

'Yes, she's gone to the ladies.'

'I'll go and get her,' said Hat. 'Hold this, Eric', and she handed me her balloon. Then the kid handed me his and ran off, and I looked a right idiot standing there with three balloons. My luck was in, however, because before Hat came back I'd sold them.

'She's not in there,' said Hat.

'That's typical, that is,' I muttered. 'Went in and had one, then completely forgot about the lad when she came out.'

'Never mind,' said Hat. 'She'll soon find us when she sees the balloons.' Then she did a double take. 'What happened to the balloons?' I told her, and we went off and had a drink at the Metropole.

The only good to come out of it all was that Corky without his contact hadn't spotted Tillie either so at least I got thirty quid back. Oh, and there was another ray of sunshine – when we got back for lunch we learned that the bathroom window had jammed. Mr Brown had been stuck on the fire escape clutching his towel to him for over an hour before somebody spotted him and opened the window. The bathroom was flooded and water had gone through the ceiling into the dining-room, and if Mr Brown hadn't been put to bed with suspected pneumonia Mrs Webb would have had him on the two o'clock train for sure.

Mercifully the week came to an end and the time came to pack our bags. Mr Brown was in a shocking state but insisted he was well enough to travel – Mrs Webb had given him such a rucking he'd have hitch-hiked home with blackwater fever rather than face her again.

Corky was looking down in the mouth. The young policeman had hobbled in with his foot in plaster to claim his half of the Tillie loot, so that put Corky more in the red because he'd already paid me thirty quid; and by the time he'd settled his bill with Mrs Webb he looked like a broken old man. I brought one of my cases down and there he was, sitting on a chair in the hall, gazing vacantly into his purse.

'Cheer up,' I said. 'It's only money.'

He looked up at me. 'It's all right for you, you get yours on the social security. I have to work for mine.'

I ignored it and went back to my bedroom. It was only then that I realized there'd been something odd about him – it suddenly struck me that he'd been so shocked by having to pay out money, he'd only remembered to black in the right half of his moustache. Viewed from one side he still bore a faint resemblance to Ronald Colman, but when he turned the other way it looked as if he had a thin strip of plaster on his top lip.

Anyway, one thing was for sure – this would be our last communal holiday and I wouldn't be sorry. I was just tying the string round my other suitcase when Jocelyn and Mrs Webb popped in. I looked up, then went on with my packing.

'Just came in to say goodbye, Ricky.'

'Goodbye, Jocelyn,' I said, without looking up.

'You've been avoiding me all week, haven't you?' It was as if she was talking to someone slightly backward.

'I haven't been avoiding you,' I said. 'A couple of days I was bedridden and the rest of the week you were always off somewhere.'

Jocelyn giggled and looked at Mrs Webb. 'Only at certain times,' she said. 'For instance: 11 and 11.30 Esplanade, 11.30 to 12 Winter Gardens, Floral Clock.' She stopped and waited.

I hoisted my suitcase off the bed, then I flung it back on again, startled. 'You are Tillie Truelove,' I blurted.

She shrieked with laughter. 'Yes, but you're too late now. You are a silly boy.'

I slumped down on the bed. What a turn-up for the book! I'd been searching and scheming and walking my feet off and she'd been right here under my nose. Sixty quid a day touching my knee under the table every mealtime, and I didn't know it. I turned and looked at her. She thought it a big joke.

'Wait a minute,' I said. 'Tillie Truelove is blonde.'

'A wig, silly,' and she took it out of a carrier bag and swung it round. 'Well, 'bye Ricky. Better luck next time,' and she blew me a kiss and was gone.

I sat there dejected. It was clear now about that day with the balloons. No wonder Jocelyn didn't come out of the toilet. She went *in* all right, but Tillie Truelove came out in a blonde wig. I sat bolt upright – and good grief, while I was standing outside holding those three balloons she'd bought one of them and I hadn't even recognized her. What an idiot I was. What a great mark one super de luxe berk I was. I realized that Mrs Webb was still standing by the door.

'Well, I'll be off now, Mrs Webb.' I shrugged philosophically. 'There's always next year.'

'Not here there isn't.' She folded her arms.

'Eh?' I looked at her blankly.

'Well, it wouldn't be fair, would it?' she said. 'Now that you know that the girl from the *Daily Bugle* stays here, you'd be able to spot her easy. I mean, I bent over backwards for you with Jocelyn, introducing you, and putting her at your table.'

'Yes, but I thought you – ' I broke off and the enormity of it all hit me. 'Mrs Webb, every year for the past twelve years we've been coming here and you – '

She nodded. 'And every year I've been introducing you to the girl, and every year you've avoided her like the plague while everybody else in Bogsea has been cashing in.'

I just stared at her, haggard and sick. 'You haven't got a couple of aspirin, have you?'

Well, that was our last holiday in Bogsea. We haven't been back since, and it's a few years now, but I still wake up sweating some nights when I think of all the fivers I threw away.

THE MARRIAGE

In the starting gate, before the steward's enquiry.

I came home the other night and I was choked. It has been one of those days that started with the dawn, then got darker. From the minute I clocked on at the factory there had been nothing but hassles, and all because of a toolbox that had gone missing. Last year the firm had a turn over of £15 million, and here they were coming the Gestapo because of a miserable toolbox. We'd all been questioned and even forced to turn out our lockers. We accepted the situation stoically, although time was going by and we were eager to get to work; in fact one man actually started his machine, but such a howl went up he quickly switched it off again.

However the mood of calm resignation suddenly changed when word went round that they would be docking our pay unless the missing toolbox was returned. That put the cat among the pigeons. The lads had a meeting and it was unanimously decided that if they docked us one penny we were out; there could be no other course open to us except industrial action. We even approached the transport section with regard to their coming out in sympathy, but unfortunately they were already out in sympathy with the packers. That shattered us completely – the transport section's first sympathy should have been with us, because only a month ago we'd been out in sympathy with them over their right to pick up hitch-hikers, and after that dispute had been settled it was tacitly agreed that they would back us in any of our grievances. Now, when we needed them, they were out with the packers of all people – half of them could hardly speak English, and six months ago their shop steward ran a bicycle shop in Bangladesh. On top of all this they were out because they claimed the stuff used in packing made them cough. Well, that's a laugh. I mean for a start they're bound to cough coming over here to our cold climate, and secondly you can't see two yards in front of you in the packing department for cigarette smoke. And the pathetic thing is the management daren't come the heavy with them or they'd be up before the race relations board.

Anyway the news that we were on our own cast a gloom over the meeting. I'd hoped we'd be back at work by this time because it was my turn to buy a round. Luckily before I could say 'Same again' the foreman walked in and told us the missing toolbox had turned up, just like that. Then he stood there looking round at us, and we just looked back at him. He repeated the news as if he expected a round of applause, or perhaps we'd sing 'For He's a Jolly Good Fellow' and there'd be a mad stampede to the factory to get our machines started up, but we'd already been through too much. He was asked politely to withdraw. Well, he was asked to withdraw. Or rather, told to withdraw – to be quite truthful Jack Cronkle told him to —. Anyway he went.

There and then we convened another meeting with regard to compensation re casting aspersions on our integrity, and by the time the pub closed we had agreed to return to work on receipt of a written apology from the management, and a shorter working week. With this motion in hand we trooped back to the factory canteen for lunch, only to find that being after two o'clock it was officially closed. Straightaway I was on a deputation to the management, because although our meeting had taken longer than anticipated we were still entitled under the Factories Act to a lunch break.

The management agreed to approach the canteen staff, so we had to hang about while negotiations went on. This was another disaster because I lost £15 in a poker game, and just when I was hitting a lucky streak a spokesman came in to tell us the canteen had agreed to open for half an hour. We later found out that in return the canteen staff got concessions of double time and an extra holiday; and also just as we walked into the canteen the whistle went for knocking off, so we went out again – nobody in his right mind eats canteen food in his own time.

That's the sort of day it was, and all because of a tool-box – there were still a couple of spanners missing but the management weren't going to make an issue out of that, and you can bet your life I wasn't going to return them. As I walked home I came to the conclusion that I was up to here with the industrial scene. I was so deep in depression I walked into Madge's bread shop. Why I walked in there I'll never really know, because normally I try to avoid her. I mean she's all right, and she makes doughnuts like you dream about, but she fancies me, and deep down in my heart I think there's something wrong with anybody who fancies me. For instance if she sees me pass the shop she'll dash out and thrust a bag of doughnuts in my hand and say: 'For my inner Ricky.' This has been going on for years, and although I'm fond of doughnuts I'd rather she delivered them to the house when I'm out. So why I walked into her shop of my own volition is beyond me.

'Ricky,' she gasped, her eyes lighting up like two currants in a suet pudding.

I smiled weakly. 'A small brown loaf please, Madge.'

'What you on about, you naughty boy? Your sister picked up the bread this morning.'

I glanced through the window across to our house, and I saw the curtain fall back into place. Hat was watching, and she'd seen me in Madge's. So what, and what was I doing here? What prompted me to walk in? I suddenly realized that Madge was leaning across the counter towards me with her eyes closed and a doughnut in her mouth, and I knew what was expected of me, but I wasn't going to bite the other half.

She opened her eyes and looked at me like a fat labrador you've just hit over the head with a shovel: 'Ont oo ike dowuts anino?', which roughly translated without a mouthful of doughnut I took to mean 'Don't you like doughnuts any more?'

'Of course I do, Madge,' and as I said it I had a blinding flash of inspiration. Most of my disasters in life have been triggered by a blinding flash of inspiration, but I never lose faith, and it occurred to me in that split second that doughnuts were the answer. After all I must be one of the greatest living experts on doughnuts, and I knew without a doubt that Madge was a genius when it came to creating them.

'What's the matter, Ricky?' she pleaded.

I ignored her and paced up and down while my imagination took hold. Brie cheese was known worldwide; Châteauneuf du Pape, Aylesbury duck – why should not Madge's doughnuts be prized worldwide? She could be another Colonel Sanders' Kentucky Fried Chicken. It only needed a man who was intelligent and willing to work at it, a man with drive and imagination, and here I was. Fate had turned my footsteps into Madge's shop. I'd be free of the factory and its disputes, labour relations and petty squabbling. Already I was planning. First I'd get Madge's doughnuts known around the district, then the country, leading into the EEC; but America was the big one – they practically lived on doughnuts out there. I stopped pacing and faced Madge.

'Oh, Ricky,' she gushed, and wobbled all over.

I looked at the sugar round her mouth and the bit of jam on her nose, and I shuddered. Was it worth it? But I dismissed the thought quickly. 'Madge,' I said. 'Your doughnuts.'

Straightaway she was on the defensive. 'What's the matter with 'em?'

'There's nothing the matter with them, Madge. They're delicious, brilliant works of art.'

She looked at me sideways, wondering if I was pulling her leg.

'Your doughnuts, Madge, are marvellous, but who buys them?'

She shrugged.

'I'll tell you who buys them – a few scruffs, just yobboes in this area, and they don't really appreciate them.'

She looked sharply at me.

'They don't Madge. I've seen them giving 'em to kids.'

I paused to give her a chance to say 'So what?', and she did.

'Listen, Madge, your doughnuts are not being exploited. You should be getting orders from all over England, you should be inundated, then there's the EEC, all the Benelux countries; now there's a market for you. Do you know they can't get doughnuts in France? They have to eat patisserie, and what's more they eat it for breakfast. They're not like us with bacon and eggs – they like patisserie. So can you imagine what they'd do with a good doughnut?'

'That's all very well,' she said, 'but I've only got one pair of hands.'

'Ah, yes. *Now* you have; but Hat's doing nothing.'

She looked at me blankly. 'I don't know what you're on about,' she said.

I leaned over the counter. 'What I'm trying to say, Madge, is this: you need someone behind you, someone to push you.'

She sniggered coyly and touched me playfully on the nose. 'Cheeky,' she said.

'I'm serious, Madge.'

She stared at me for a moment, then she placed her

hands flatly on the counter and her eyes went dull. 'You're playing a game with me aren't you? You're having a bit of fun.'

I shook my head. 'I'm not, Madge, honestly. If I wanted a bit of fun I wouldn't be here, would I?'

She jerked upright.

'What I mean is, well you probably think I'm a bit pushy, but – er – well, I'm not going to beat about the bush. What it boils down to is, why don't you and me go into partnership?'

Her mouth fell open, and a split second later her top dentures sagged, but being a gentleman I turned away. 'Fartnershiff', she croaked, too stunned to realize that her top set was still out of kilter.

I picked up a loaf and pretended to examine it so she could adjust herself.

'You and me in partnership?' she said, and I knew it was safe to look at her.

'Why not? The way you make doughnuts, and my brains, it's a natural combination.'

Her eyes glistened and I knew I had her.

I went on: 'It's funny, isn't it,' I said. 'You look for something all your life, and here it is on your own doorstep.'

A tear rolled down her cheek, and she brushed it away leaving a black smear. 'Oh, Ricky! I'll have to think it over,' she blubbed, and wiped mascara down her other cheek.'

'That's it, Madge,' I said, and patted her hand. 'Think it over.' Then I hurried out of the shop – I didn't want anybody catching me in there. What with the jam on her nose, the sugar and the black cheeks, she was beginning to look like a Picasso.

Hat wasn't too excited when I told her the news; in fact she was decidedly lukewarm. 'How can you buy half of Madge's shop?' she said. 'You need bread for that.' Then, realizing what she'd said, she fell back laughing. 'You need bread for that,' she spluttered.

I looked at her coldly.

'Don't you get it Eric? *Bread*.'

I turned away and I knew how Michelangelo must have felt dashing home excited to tell his mother: 'Mamma mia, they want me – Michelangelo – to paint the Sistine Chapel.'

And his mother calmly doing her tapestry, saying: 'Well, before you start that, the back bedroom wants doing.'

Hat had finished laughing now, but I could see she was wondering who she could tell it to.

'I'm not buying the shop,' I said. 'I'm merely going into partnership with her.'

She was scornful. 'You in a bread shop,' You can't even make toast.'

'I won't be actually in the bread shop as such, will I? I'll be Head of Sales.'

'Oh,' she said. 'A delivery boy.'

'Listen, Hat. I know it's only a small bread shop now, but it's a goldmine. Madge's doughnuts, I mean you can't beat 'em. You know how good they are – I bought you one for your birthday. Remember? With a candle in the middle. And you said then, if they weren't so fattening you could eat them morning, noon and night.'

'It wasn't much of a birthday present, was it? After all, I bought you a thermal vest.'

'Never mind the birthdays,' I snapped. 'Madge is a genius, but no business sense. Well, that's where I come in. I intend to put her doughnuts on the map.' And with that I made to go upstairs.

'Has Madge agreed to this?'

I leaned over the banister. 'How can she refuse? She won't turn her nose up at a fur coat and a few million in the bank, not to mention the Queen's Award.'

As I ran the bath I felt good about that Queen's Award bit. If there was any hesitation on Madge's part that would swing it. She was very pro-royal, as we all were – she'd even taken a bag of doughnuts to the palace on the Queen's Jubilee, but she'd had to leave them with the policeman on the gate. And here I take my hat off to our police: he said he would deliver them personally as soon as he'd walked the Corgis. I lay back happily in the warm, sudsy water, oblivious to the dark storm clouds gathering. Half an hour later I was still in a semi-comatose state in the bath while downstairs Hat was opening the door to a freshly made-up and breathless Madge.

'Oh hello, Madge. Come in. Would you like some tea? I'm just having a cup.'

Madge smiled and sat down on the edge of the chair, as if she was waiting to see the doctor.

Hat pointed to the ceiling. 'Eric's in the bath.'

Madge blushed at the thought. Hat handed her a cup of tea, and settled down on the settee. They smiled at each other, then looked down at their cups, then they looked at each other and smiled again. Hat decided to jump in at the deep end.

'Eric's told me all about it.'

Madge spluttered on a mouthful of tea. Here was Hattie coming straight to the nub of the matter, and they hadn't even discussed the weather. She put her cup on the table and joined Hat on the settee. 'Hattie,' she started. 'You may not believe this, but I never said a word. The first I knew of it was this evening.'

'That's all right, Madge. But are you sure – I mean really sure – you're doing the right thing? After all, Eric hasn't had a lot of experience.'

'I know that, Hattie. But that's what makes it right because . . .' and here she looked away, '. . . well, to tell you the truth I haven't had many chances either.'

Hat put her arm round her. 'But don't you see, Madge? That shop is your whole life.'

'I know, and I want to share it with Eric.' She looked

earnestly at Hat. 'You don't mind, do you? What I mean is, he always led me to believe that you were against him getting married.'

It was Hat's turn to splutter – well, splutter is hardly the word; a jet of tea shot across the room that would have done credit to a fully grown whale. Madge pumped her vigorously on the back. Hat struggled to her feet, fighting for breath. 'Sorry, Madge,' she gasped. 'I thought you said "married".'

Madge blushed. 'Isn't it marvellous? I've always felt that doughnuts were half an excuse to see me, but I never thought he'd ever get serious.'

Hat flopped back on the settee. 'Married? He actually asked you?'

'Yes. Typical Eric, he didn't come straight out with it, he said a partnership for life – well, you know what he's like.'

Hat blew her nose.

'Don't worry, Hattie. I'll take care of him, I promise.'

Hat turned to her and took her hands. 'Madge, are you sure that that's what he meant – I mean to get married?'

Madge smiled. 'It's not what he said, it was in his eyes . . . he's never looked at me like that before.'

Hat tried again. 'Yes I know, Madge – .'

But Madge wasn't listening. She broke in: 'Hattie, you know what people round here are like. Let's keep it dark for the time being. Let's not mention it to anybody.'

Hat shook her head sadly. 'I think we should tell Eric.' And at that moment I made an appearance down the stairs.

'Hello, Madge,' I said. 'Thought it over yet?'

Madge bounced off the settee and flung herself at me. 'Ricky, oh Ricky,' and she gave me a kiss on the cheek. Well, I say a kiss, but it wasn't human. I made a mental note that next time our sink was blocked to hell with the plumber, I'd send for Madge. I looked up into her face, and that was odd because I'm taller than she is; then I realized she was wearing her corsets, and they tend to take her in at the middle and add nine inches to her height.

'For goodness sake, Madge,' I gasped. 'I haven't had my tea yet.'

She let me go then, and minced to a chair. 'Tell me again what you said in the shop.'

'Yes, go on, Eric. Tell her again,' said Hat, and handed me a tumbler half full of whisky.

I stared at her in amazement. Hat doesn't mind me having the odd night out with the lads or even pouring myself a snifter at home providing I'm not well, but she has never ever poured me a drink of her own free will, except for that time when I fell off my bike, and then she rubbed it on my leg. I raised the glass to Madge and said: 'Here's to us.'

'Oh, Ricky,' she said, and sniffed into a minute hankie. That took some of the powder off, and there she was with a red nose again. She reminded me of an overdressed snowman with a cherry in the middle of its face. I knew then that I was going to have to earn my first million, and resolved to spend most of my time on sales trips abroad.

I took a sip of whisky, and it caught me in the back of the throat. Hat hadn't even put water in it. She led me to a chair. 'I think you'd better sit,' she said. 'I don't want you hurting yourself when you fall down.'

I looked at her quizzically. 'On one drink?'

'It's not the drink I'm worried about,' she said, and inclined her head meaningfully towards Madge.

Something stirred in my bowels, and it wasn't just the whisky. I looked across at Madge and she was sitting on the edge of the chair leaning forwards eagerly bright button eyes watching my every move. I swear if I'd thrown a stick she would have fetched it.

Hat jogged my elbow. 'Go on,' she said. 'Tell us again what you said in the shop.'

I pulled myself together. 'The first thing we've got to

do, Madge, is put your doughnuts on the map.' I wasn't sure, but I thought I saw some of the eagerness go out of her eyes. I pressed on. 'While I was having a bath just now it came to me. We have to use the media: TV commercials, that's the hammer.' I started to pace up and down. 'You've seen chocolate ads on the telly, haven't you? Adverts for nuts, cream, pork sausages. But when have you ever seen one for doughnuts?' I looked at them both triumphantly.

Madge looked at me earnestly. 'I'm going to try to make you happy, Ricky.'

I leaned forward, hands on the table. 'And I'm going to make you happy too, Madge.'

I could see she was about to get up and probably leap at me again, so I quickly resumed my pacing. 'A doughnut commercial,' I said, 'and it has to hit 'em.' Out of the corner of my eye I noticed with relief that she'd settled again. 'And what sells a commercial? Come on, what sells a commercial?' I didn't expect an answer, so I carried on: 'Sex.'

They both blushed.

'No. Face up to it,' I said, 'It's sex. There's always a pretty girl in it; a fellow smoking a pipe, and there's always a girl next to him going "Ooooh"; then there's the "Oh mummy, what makes your hands so soft?" That's not her mother, it's a dolly bird, and they're only selling detergent.'

Hat nodded in agreement. 'If they're advertising cars, it's always a pretty girl that gets in and drives off.'

'Right,' I said. 'And I bet if it was a surgical truss some Lulu would hold it against her cheek and say, "He never wears anything else." '

'I've never seen that one,' said Hat.

I shook my head impatiently. 'I'm speaking hypothetically, but I'll tell you something – if it was advertised there'd be many a fit young man walking around in a surgical truss, so they could impress their girlfriends.'

'It costs money to put on a commercial,' said Madge.

'Ah yes, but all depending on how expensive you want to go. I mean if you want Sophia Loren lying on a beach in the Bahamas eating a doughnut it'll set you back a bit, but this is what I had in mind. . . .' I was so wrapped up in my thoughts I pulled my chair closer to Madge and I didn't even notice her put her hand on my knee. 'We can get a camera anywhere – that's no problem – then we can shoot the commercial right here in this house.'

Hat looked round the room sceptically.

'Listen. We shoot it close, a young couple sitting at a table – ' I made a square with my finger as if I was looking through a television set. 'We zoom in – chequered cloth, mandolines playing in the background, a bottle of Chianti and we could be in the south of France.'

Madge cleared her throat. 'Ricky, you are Church of England, aren't you?'

I looked at her puzzled. I couldn't see how two people sitting at a table smiling at a doughnut could possibly be blasphemous.

Hat answered the question. 'Oh yes, we're Church of England and always have been.'

Madge nodded. 'That's all right, then. I knew you weren't Catholic, because they're usually ardent and I've never seen you go to church. I mean, you don't have to go to church if you're C of E, but Catholics are very strict on that sort of thing.'

Hat was quick to agree. 'Too strict, if you ask me. I mean Eric and I used to go to church before they had *Stars on Sunday*, and then we lapsed, but even so the vicar will always give you a "Good morning" or raise his hat. Whatsisname, Eric? Er – Reverend something.'

Madge shook her head. 'I've never met him. I'm chapel myself, on the corner of Balaclava Road.'

'Oh yes, I know it,' said Hat. 'It's a bingo hall now.'

Madge's mouth fell open. 'Fancy! I never knew that.'

Hat leaned forward to Madge. 'Have you noticed the young Catholic priest who calls on the McNamaras?'

Madge's lips pursed. 'I know the one, red-faced and always has a boil going on the back of his neck.'

'That's the one,' said Hat. 'He always has a sort of musty smell – religious. Know what I mean?'

Madge nodded sagely. 'It's unction water.'

I coughed for attention. 'Can we shelve the theological discussion till later. After all, I can't see what its got to do with me and Madge.'

They both looked at each other conspiratorially, then Hat turned to me. 'Go on, Eric. There's this young couple sitting at a table in the south of France?'

I spoke uncertainly. 'Thats it, with a bottle of Chianti.' I stopped. Surely it couldn't be unction water; unction had something to do with ointment.

Hat brought me out of my reverie. 'Go on, Eric.' She was looking at me in a strange way, as if I was her eight-year-old son doing well in a talent contest.

I pressed on. 'Well, there's this couple, you see, soft candlelight, the man leans across the table, takes a box out of his pocket like an engagement ring. She opens it, and instead of a ring it's a doughnut.'

I stood back waiting for a reaction, it wasn't exactly encouraging. Hat said: 'Would you like some more tea?' and Madge said: 'No, thank you.'

'What d'you think?' I said. 'A great little commercial, and so far it's cost us nothing.'

'Actors aren't cheap, you know,' said Hat. 'David Niven got £50,000 for coffee beans.'

I sauntered to the window and looked out. 'I wasn't thinking of David Niven. What's wrong with me doing it?'

There was a snigger and I whipped round, but they were both looking at the floor. 'I won't cost anything. Well, a token fee – and we can soon find a young dolly bird who'll give her eye teeth to be on the telly.'

'In that case you're not playing the man,' snapped Madge.

Hat was examining her fingernails. The silence was so dense I wondered why the clock hadn't driven me mad before now. Then somewhere close by I heard the plaintive cry of a lonely cat, but then Madge went beetroot red and I realized it was her stomach acting up.

Hat broke the silence. 'It's all very well, Eric, but you can't just go on telly like that. You have to be an actor.'

'Wrong,' I said, and played my ace. 'Not when you're advertising your own product. Look at Freddie Laker – he does his own commercial, and I've never seen him top the bill at the National Theatre.'

Hat jumped in eagerly. 'Well then, Madge can play the girl.'

Madge brightened.

I tried to make light of it. 'Well, not really. The doughnut is supposed to be an engagement between two people having dinner, it's not a plug for meals on wheels.'

'Thank you very much,' said Madge. 'I'll remember that remark.'

I tried to mollify her. 'I'm not getting at you, Madge, but you haven't really done anything in the acting line, have you? And I mean, with all due respect, I was in *The Pirates of Penzance.*'

Hat looked sharply at me, but I flashed her a warning glance. I hadn't actually told a lie, but being with the local amateur operatic society as a scene shifter doesn't carry the same ring of authority.

'What I'm trying to say, Madge, is this. The doughnut commercial isn't finalized. It's just off the top of my head and – '

She broke in impatiently: 'Yes, yes. I know all that, Ricky. I appreciate the way you think, I've always admired you for your mind – there isn't a week goes by without Hattie telling me how you're thinking about things and that. But what I'm saying is, first things first.'

'I agree, Madge,' I said. 'I'm sorry I was so far ahead of you, but as you say, I have a brain like quicksilver. I mean, in my mind I've already got a chain of doughnut stands all over the Middle West, while you're still wondering if you've left the gas on.'

'Oh Ricky, what I mean is – ', but I silenced her.

'As you say, Madge, first things first. We put the doughnuts in coloured bags – '

Madge sprang to her feet. 'Bugger the doughnuts, Ricky. What about us?'

There was a stunned silence. Hat quickly glanced out of the window to see if anyone was passing. Madge looked wildly at me, then dissolved in a flood of tears. I didn't know what to do. I floundered helplessly. I mean, I can go a bit when I'm with the lads, but I never swear at home.

'I'm sorry,' she blubbed. 'I didn't mean to say that, but you will keep on about my doughnuts.' Her voice rose. 'But what about *us*, you and me?'

'I'm coming to that, Madge', I said coldly, desperately trying to regain control, but also to let her know that as master in my own house I didn't condone bad language. 'Now,' I continued. 'We put the doughnuts in coloured bags, and on every bag in big letters we have the name Sykes and Kettlewell Ltd.'

She stared at me blankly.

'Well, I mean, Madge – it sounds better than Kettlewell and Sykes Ltd, and you have to think of these things.'

She looked at me coyly, finger going round the top of her teacup. 'What about Sykes and Son Ltd?' She sniffed.

It was my turn to stand open-mouthed, I looked at Hat, but she was no help. She just raised her eyebrows at me as if to say 'Follow that', and strolled to the window, whistling tunelessly to herself. I knew that affected nonchalance of Hat's; it usually presages me going into the cart head first.

I probed gently: 'Sykes and Son Ltd?'

Madge sat upright. 'I'm not too old, you know.' She blushed again.

I shrugged at Hat for enlightenment, but she was still pretending to gaze idly out of the window. Her hands were going pat-pat-pat behind her back, another tell-tale sign meaning 'Get out of that'. The warning bells which had been going in my head for some time were louder now – not only warning bells but flashing lights, sirens and fog-horns. Madge broke the spell.

'You do like children, don't you, Ricky?'

'Of course I like children, Madge,' I said fervently, and I believed it. I do like children as long as they don't get too close.

Madge took hold of my hand and looked directly into my eyes. 'And if for some reason or other we're not blessed, we can always adopt one.'

A trickle of perspiration ran from my armpit – adopt a child? That's a bit like having a hangover without the pleasure of getting stoned. She squeezed my fingers and I winced. The thought flashed across my mind that had I been a violinist there'd be no performance that night. 'You can't adopt a child just like that, Madge. You have to be married.'

'Isn't that what you want, Ricky?' she said softly.

I snatched my hand away. 'Married?' I gulped.

'It wasn't my idea, you naughty boy. It was you who came into my shop and proposed.'

The whole jigsaw fell into place in one horrific moment. I reached automatically for the bottle, but Hat was already pouring me one. 'Married,' I said, as if it was a new word in the dictionary. 'Listen, Madge. I'm offering you a chance to make millions, shops all over the world, cars, mink coats, but I'll have to concentrate. Good grief, you should know it doesn't pay to mix business with – ' I stopped short and looked at her, and I couldn't bring myself to say 'pleasure'. I tried a reasonable approach. 'You know, Madge, much as

I'd like it, let's shelve the marriage.' She half rose, so I rushed on: '. . . for the time being.' She settled down again. 'First of all let me make you internationally famous, Madge, and when I've made you a millionaire then we'll talk about marriage. After all, Madge, I have my pride. I don't want to come to you with nothing.' I looked at her earnestly.

'Ricky, oh Ricky. I have a little bit put by – it'll be enough to see things through.'

I turned away. 'It's a tempting thought, Madge, but I'm going to be strong for both of us. If I married you on that basis it would dog me for the rest of my days – a kept man.'

'But Ricky, once we're married you'll be able to go ahead with those marvellous ideas of yours, putting the doughnuts in coloured bags and things.'

I shook my head sadly. 'I have to be honest with you, Madge. There's always a risk in business – for instance, let's suppose that my ideas didn't work out. There's always that possibility, you know.'

She came to me and spoke softly. 'Yes, Ricky, but we'd be married.'

I gulped another drink to disguise the spasm of revulsion that must have swept my face. I tried another tack. 'Look, Madge, if I was an ordinary sort of bloke – you know, Mr Average, dull, mundane – I'd marry you like a shot, because let's face it, Madge – you're a good catch.'

Hat looked over her shoulder at me, but apart from that she just stood by and listened to me digging a big pit for myself. Madge just sat stony-faced.

I began to pace up and down in the hope that somebody else would say something. Why didn't I just come right out and say, 'I'm sorry, Madge, forget the marriage'? But I wasn't sure of her reaction, and I'd already felt that grip of hers; if it became more physical I could be marked for life, on top of which all my schemes of selling doughnuts to the jet set would come to nothing. As I thought about this I realized that already I was going lukewarm on the idea. I tried again.

'Look, Madge, marriage isn't just a question of saying I do and handing over a couple of quid to the registrar. There's more to it than that. There's emotions involved.'

Hat gave an 'Oh my God' look at the ceiling, but Madge still sat there, mouth set like a tiny minus sign.

I slumped into a chair, feeling very old. I thought about my marvellous scheme with distaste. Who wants to fly about all over the place, living out of a suitcase, eating foreign food? I had better things to do with my life than dashing from door to door with a bag of doughnuts. My thoughts went longingly to the factory – the banter and comradeship of the lads, the fun we had with the packers, who weren't a bad lot of coloureds. I took another swig of my whisky, and I thought of the day the foreman took me to see the nursing sister when Clydesdale dropped that monkey wrench on my foot – fatherly but firm, as a good foreman should be, and the board room – they were a pretty decent lot, and it wasn't their fault they happened to be in management. I realized that Madge was talking.

'Well, Ricky, what is it to be? A wedding, or is this it?'

'Madge,' I started, but she was in no mood for reasonable debate.

'I want to know, Ricky, because if the wedding's off I'll have to phone cousin Rupert.'

The name hit me in the stomach. I'd seen Rupert several times, but only in the newspapers, either full face and wanted, an identikit picture suspect, or being hustled into a side door with a blanket over his head. Madge often brought him up in the conversation and talked as if she was a bit ashamed of him, but I reckoned if you were ashamed of something you kept quiet about it, and I figured she used him as a deterrent. I felt trapped.

'What's your cousin Rupert got to do with it?' I asked, although I knew the answer.

She blushed a little. 'I don't have much family, so I felt I had to ask him to the wedding,' she said.

'When?' I asked.

'Just before I came out I phoned him.'

Hat turned from the window. 'And what date did you have in mind for the wedding?' she asked in a strange voice.

Madge shrugged. 'Well, I don't know how long these things take. I mean the registrar was very nice, and took our names and things – '

I struggled to my feet. The whisky was making me reckless. 'You gave our names?' I said. 'I don't mind you giving your name, but you've no right to give mine – it's private.'

Madge looked at me helplessly. 'Well, he asked me, didn't he? And you have to give him names. I mean, he can't stand up with a blindfold on and say "Do you, Mr X, take Miss Y for your lawfully wedded wife".' She spread her hands and appealed to Hat, then she came over to me and smiled. What I mean is, I assumed she was smiling but her face was slightly out of focus, and it was the kind of look one has when one is trying to unscrew a tight bottle top. Her voice came from a long way off. 'You'll thank me when we're sunning ourselves on the beach at Majorca.'

'Majorca – ', I repeated, with effort.

Again her voice floated to me from outer space: 'Week in Majorca for our honeymoon. I'll get the tickets tomorrow.'

I began to get angry. 'You haven't been dragging your feet, have you?' I said.

Madge's amicable expression fell off, and I had a quick flash of Rupert coming up the street with a couple of heavies, but the whisky kept me going.

'Well, good grief, Madge. I just shop into your pop to talk about – ' I stopped suddenly. I realized that I'd said 'shop into your pop' and I hoped they hadn't noticed it. I carried on carefully. 'I pop into your shop this afternoon to talk about doughnuts, and all of a sudden I'm an old married man.'

Hat spoke nonchalantly: 'Adam took the apple.'

I swung my gaze round to her. It passed her slightly, then swung back and docked. 'Don't give me that. I'm a very eligible bachelor, whereas Adam didn't have a lot of choice, did he? So don't start quoting the scriptures to me, madam. Don't forget I was the one who nearly went into a monastery.'

Hat stifled a smile. My thoughts tumbled back to that period in my life when I was about to reject society. In fact I'd already written off to Newton Abbot, but then I saw a TV documentary where they showed the monks getting up at four o'clock in the morning, and that put me off. I realized that Madge was talking again.

'What's it to be, Ricky?'

I slumped down in the chair. 'OK, Madge. You want an answer, and I'll give you one. I'll agree to marriage only on certain terms.'

'Oh, Ricky,' she gushed. 'Anything you say,' and knelt down in front of me, which was a reckless thing to do because I was in no condition to help her up again.

'Right, Hat. Get a notebook and pen and you'll be a witness. OK?'

Hat took a notebook out of the drawer and sat down next to me rather anxiously.

'One,' I said. She wrote down 'one'. 'My sister Hattie will come with us on our honeymoon.'

Hat glanced sharply at Madge, then wrote it down.

Madge gaped. 'Oh, Ricky. I've only arranged tickets for two.'

'Well then, you and Hat go,' I said.

Hat protested, but I held up my hand for silence.

'It'll do you good. You need a change.'

Madge struggled to her feet like an elephant with Cyril Smith in the howdah. She straightened her skirt. 'If you don't go, I'm not going either,' she said.

I looked at Hat. 'OK, Hat, it's you and me. We could do with a holiday.'

'I won't be a party to it,' snapped Madge.

'OK then, baby. That's the marriage out. Now, any other business?'

Madge was contrite. 'No, I mean we'll just cancel the honeymoon. We don't have to have one.'

I realized she was backing down and my confidence increased. I turned to Hat: 'No honeymoon.' She dutifully jotted it down. I looked up at the ceiling for inspiration. 'Clause two . . .', I waited till the pencil stopped. 'Although Madge Kettlewell and I the above-mentioned will be married . . .', I waited to let Hat catch up. 'Although Madge etc. etc. will be married, I will continue to live here with my aforementioned sister Harriet.'

At this they were both at me. 'Oh, no', 'Wait a minute', 'Hang on', etc.

I held up my arms. 'OK, OK. I'll amend that to four nights a week.'

Hat looked at Madge, and Madge said: 'Four nights a week?'

'Yes, and that doesn't include club night and bingo.'

'Oh, Rick.'

Hat wrote 'club night and bingo'. I was beginning to focus better and I had the feeling I was in complete command of the situation. 'Clause three' – Madge was pacing up and down now so I pressed on quickly. 'During which times I shall be domiciled at Madge's etc. etc. we shall have separate bedrooms.'

Madge stopped in her tracks. 'Separate bedrooms?'

'Separate bedrooms,' I replied, 'and with locks.'

Hat stared at me in amazement. She's always thought of me as a kindly gentle person. It wouldn't do her any harm to glimpse the tiger in me now and again.

Madge stepped forward: 'No woman in her right mind would accept these terms.'

I eyed her coldly for a moment. 'Well, Madge. That's it.'

Her fists clenched and the veins came up on her neck.

'That's it, is it?' she hissed. 'That's it.' Her voice strengthened. 'No honeymoon, sleep here, club nights and bingo.' She flounced to the door and flung it open, and she turned, breathing heavily, her big chest going up and down. I wondered how the buttons in front managed to hold things together. In a sarcastic tone of voice she said: 'Will it be alright if I give you a kiss on the cheek every Christmas?' Then she went and slammed the door so hard that two pictures fell down.

We sat in silence for a moment, then Hat started to pick up *The Stag at Bay*. 'Well,' she said, 'you got out of that', and I felt there was a note of admiration in the way she said it.

I stood up and smiled grimly at her. 'Don't worry, Hat, you have to be up early to get one over on this kiddie.' I swirled the whisky in the glass and drained it. 'She doesn't frighten me with Rupert,' I said. 'I'm not a violent man, Hat, but you've never really seen me when I'm roused.'

She looked at me over her shoulder. I put the glass down and thumped a fist into the palm of my hand. 'Let Rupert come the old GBH with me, and it'll be Goodnight Vienna.' I went to do a karate kick but unfortunately my foot caught in the rug and I fell over the settee.

Hat looked at me gravely. 'Eric, you're drunk,' she said.

'I'm not drunk. If you *will* leave rugs lying about all over the floor – '

Then the phone rang. Hat said: 'Hello? Oh hello, Madge. Yes, but . . . yes, but – ' She put the phone down, then turned to me slowly. 'Madge has agreed to your terms.'

I lay back on the rug and groaned, and that's where I found myself in the morning with a blanket over me.

So three weeks later I found myself sitting in the front pew at St Bartholomew's in a morning suit, and heavily sedated. Corky sat next to me in his number one uniform, a row of medals and white gloves. He was to be my best man. It had been a twilight three weeks blurred by scotch, although I vaguely remember two escape attempts and an appeal to the doctor to have me certified medically unfit for marriage. Nevertheless here I was in the condemned seat – pale, aloof, half-cut and holding onto a billiard cue. That night I was in the semi-finals of the snooker competition and I intended, come what may, to stick rigidly to my contract, and tonight at eight o'clock I'd be hot favourite to go into the finals. The vicar looked at his watch, then sauntered over with his white wedding face on. He coughed discreetly and asked me wouldn't I be more comfortable if I left the cue in the vestry, to which I replied no I wouldn't. I could imagine the spotty choirboys belting the living daylights out of each other, which would scarcely do the cue much good.

He smiled apologetically. 'They're usually a bit late,' he said. 'A bride's prerogative.' He coughed discreetly again, and withdrew.

I fervently hoped she was late. I had a sudden vision of the headlines: 'The late Miss Kettlewell on the day she was to be married . . . Miss Madge Kettlewell stepped under a bus while making her way to church.' I broke off the thought guiltily, but my thoughts had a habit of escalating . . . 'Her bridegroom-to-be, Mr Eric Sykes, amateur snooker champion, was heartbroken. Condolences have been pouring in: Cliff Thorburn said "I hope it doesn't affect his game", whilst Hurricane Higgins is reported to have said "He was always a hard man to beat, and I know he will bear his great loss as the champion he will undoubtedly become." ' I was in the middle of a eulogy from Ray Reardon when I realised that Corky was speaking.

'The bride's always late,' he said. 'It's part of the trick, you see. They can't wait to get you to the altar, then the minute you're there, *wallop*, the shackles go on and you work to their tempo.'

I ignored him. It was at Madge's insistence that he was best man – it was insurance against me skiving off, and I know for a fact that had I shown the slightest inclination to scarper he wouldn't have hesitated to use the handcuffs. In return he's on the 'free' list at Madge's bread shop. How can I respect a man who'll sell out his friend for a handful of doughnuts? On top of all this, I wasn't impressed by his performance at our house before we left. It was about 2.30, and I was sitting there washing down a few Librium with a glass of whisky, when there was a knock on the door, it was a knock I didn't recognize – it wasn't Madge's coy tit-tit, and it wasn't Corky's jocular rat-tat-tat-tat-tat – tat-tat, nor Mr Brown's peremptory command. This was two thumps with the side of a fist that jarred the glass against my teeth. Hat timidly opened the door and in came this man, not all that tall, but chunky. His face had had more stitches in it than my old trousers.

He nodded expressionlessly. 'Rupert,' he said.

I slowly got to my feet while Hat introduced herself. Then she told him who I was. He just nodded and sat down.

Hat gulped: 'Would you like a cup of tea?' she asked tentatively.

To my great, surprise, he nodded again. 'Lebbod wid doh sugar,' he said.

'Lemon?' said Hat, startled. He just looked at her and she scurried into the kitchen.

Immediately I felt embarrassed with my glass of scotch, and the bottle on the table. I motioned towards it. 'Medicine,' I said, with an apologetic smile. 'It's for my leg.' Then I limped to another seat as far away from him as possible.

His eyes never left me and I noticed several bulges in his double-breasted jacket – a revolver? rope? a hatchet? He could have anything concealed in there, or perhaps he was just a lumpy person. Hat came in with the tea. He nodded at her and took the cup, which looked the size of a thimble in his hand.

The silence was broken by rat-tat-tat-tat-tat – tat-tat, and Corky arrived. 'Well, well, well! And how's the happy bridegroom today?' He smiled hugely and rubbed his gloved hands together.

As soon as Rupert saw the uniform he casually got up and pretended to poke the fire, which incidentally wasn't even lit. All the time he was watching Corky through the mirror over the mantelpiece.

Hat smiled nervously. 'You haven't met Madge's cousin Rupert, have you?'

Corky smiled. 'I haven't had that pleasure, sir.' He stepped forward a pace, then stopped dead in his tracks as if he'd walked into an electrified fence. 'Rupert', he croaked.

Rupert turned and evidently decided there was no threat, so he put the poker down and resumed his seat.

Corky was white and dithering, and seemed to be having difficulty in knowing what to do with his hands. 'Pleased to know you,' he flushed. 'Course I'm not in your line. Traffic control, me.' He smiled nervously. 'All the lads at the station have a great respect for you – professional, that's what you are, and they all respect that. And if there's anything I can do anytime I – er,' he floundered and wiped his mouth on his handkerchief. 'Anything at all, Constable Turnbull's the name, and your cousin Madge she'll tell you, always keep a special eye on her shop, don't I, Hattie?'

Hat turned away. Even she couldn't stand this abject grovelling. I'm sure if Rupert had said 'Lie down while I walk all over you', Corky would have said 'certainly, sir', and not only would he be smiling as Rupert walked over him, he'd be guiding his feet.

'Anybody round here will tell you I'm more of a father figure than a constable.' He wiped his lips again. 'Don't forget, anything I can do, if you're ever in this district, park where you like, I'll sort it out and if there isn't a place give us a ring and I'll have somebody towed away.'

I looked at him searchingly. He wasn't joking – if Rupert

parked anywhere in this district, when he returned to drive away the car would not only be ticket-free, but washed, waxed and polished. Fortunately the wedding car arrived at that moment, which saved the constable further embarrassment, and here we were now at St Bartholomew's

Meanwhile at 28 Sebastopol Terrace Madge was parading up and down in her wedding dress, a glass of gin in her hand and a flush to her cheeks that showed it wasn't her first.

'Do you like it?' she primped.

Rupert, on his fifth cup of tea with 'lebbod', put a finger inside his collar impatiently.

'It looks lovely, Madge,' said Hat, 'but I really think we ought to go now.'

'Oh, he'll wait a bit. I've waited long enough.' She drained her glass and poured another one.

Hat looked at the clock: five past three – they were twenty minutes late already. 'It's all very well, Madge, but you don't know Eric. He'll only wait so long.'

Madge smiled secretly. 'And you don't know me,' she said. 'Constable Turnbull's looking after him, and he knows which side his bread's buttered on. Ricky will be there when I arrive if the constable has to nail his feet to the floor.'

Rupert fidgeted. 'Cub od, Badge. I've got work to do.'

Hat nodded. 'Yes, come on, Madge. How do you think Eric feels sitting there?'

Madge pondered, then she knocked back the gin and poured another. Rupert and Hat exchanged glances and she giggled. 'He'll be all right,' said Madge. 'I'll make it up to him this evening. We'll have a lovely party.'

Hat was on her feet. 'Oh no, Madge. You can't tonight, it's his club night.'

Madge's face fell. 'He's not going to abide by those stupid rules, is he?'

Hat looked at her straight. 'Well, he will tonight. He's in the semi-finals of the snooker championship.'

Madge appealed to Rupert. 'But he can't play snooker tonight.'

Rupert looked away. 'I like sdooker.'

Three miles away, at St Bartholomew's, Corky and I had just sat through our third wedding. The vicar came back up the aisle, brushing confetti from his surplice. He cleared his throat. 'I wonder – shouldn't you give your bride a ring?'

Corky patted his breast pocket. 'Don't worry, vicar. I've got that here.'

The vicar was perplexed for a moment, then he pulled himself together. 'No. I mean, shouldn't you telephone and see what's happened?'

'Oh,' smiled Corky. 'I thought you meant the ring. Yes, of course. I'll phone right away.'

But as he rose I pushed him back in the pew: 'Let sleeping dogs lie,' I said, and he gave me a worried nod.

At home the gin bottle was reaching the end of its life, and Madge was beginning to feel the effects. She had a pale sheen of sweat over her face, and her hair had collapsed.

Hat patted her hand. 'Come on, Madge,' she said. 'It's five o'clock. We really should be making a move.'

Madge dabbed away the tears. 'It's stupid,' she cried. 'I mean, after all – what's more important, me or the snooker?'

Hat took a strand of hair from Madge's mouth. 'Well, look at it this way,' she said. 'You've got the rest of your life.'

Madge rounded on her. 'Yes, apart from four nights a week he spends here. Then there's club nights and bingo.' She turned to Rupert for support.

''e's a 'ard bad', he said. 'Wud of the lads, 'e is', he said admiringly.

Madge looked at him in amazement. 'But I'll hardly ever see him,' she wailed.

Hat stepped in. 'Well, knowing Eric, I think that could prove a blessing.'

Madge sat there for a moment, then her hand flew to her mouth. Hat helped her upstairs to the bathroom.

In my reverie at St Bartholomew's I had just put away the blue and pink, and I was about to pot the black when somebody jogged my elbow, I shot upright to appeal, and found myself staring into the vicar's face. I looked about me. What was I doing here in church? Was somebody dead?

Then the vicar spoke. 'I really don't think your bride will be coming now,' he said. 'It's after 9.30.'

I stared at Corky. '9.30 at night?' I said.

He nodded.

'I don't think she'll be coming now,' repeated the vicar gently.

I stared at him. Corky helped me to my feet, and he walked me down the aisle. He said: 'Shock, you know.'

The vicar nodded sadly.

Corky went on: 'I've seen it happen often in my business – the police, you know.'

The vicar's eyes widened as if it had suddenly dawned on him that Corky was a constable.

'It's the same look when the governor comes in and says your reprieve's come through.'

The vicar nodded uncomprehendingly, and watched as we left the church.

Corky took me as far as our gate, then said he had to change to go on duty, but I knew he was dead scared of meeting Rupert again. He needn't have worried – Rupert had gone hours ago. There was Hat sitting on the settee with Madge wearing her dressing-gown. As I closed the door behind me, Madge got up and rushed over.

'Oh, Ricky,' she cried. 'Can you ever forgive me.'

I looked over her shoulder at Hat, and Hat heaved a big sigh. I threw my top hat on to a chair and walked to the whisky bottle. 'You might have sent a note round to the church,' I said.

'I'm sorry, Ricky. I know how you must be feeling.'

I poured a glass of scotch. 'How can you know how I feel?' I said. 'You haven't the foggiest idea. Everything I've worked for, strived for, dreamed about – just wiped away like that.' I made a sweeping motion with my hand, and gulped down the whisky.

'Oh, Ricky,' sobbed Madge. 'I didn't know you felt as strongly as that.'

I turned on her. 'Oh, you didn't? Oh, my one chance, and you cancel it out like that.'

Hat stared at me.

Madge touched my shoulder. 'I've said I'm sorry, Ricky.'

'It's a bit late now, isn't it, Madge? Good grief, I could have beaten Tom Butterworth easy.'

'Tom Butterworth.' said Hat.

'Yes, you know him. He's no good under pressure, and if I could have got a couple of early reds and blacks he'd have gone to pieces.'

The penny dropped. Hat nodded. 'Oh yes, you've missed the semi-finals.'

'What did you think I was talking about?' I snapped.

Madge turned away. 'Well, I'll go and get dressed, then,' she said in a small voice, and Hat went upstairs with her.

That's two months ago now, and Madge is back to her normal suffocating self, and I'm still one of the cogs in industry, but water never flows over a rock without leaving a deposit. Rupert is back in the Scrubs, but every month Hat packs a parcel of goodies and sets off on a visit. Perhaps my troubles are just beginning.